But It's Your Family

But It's Your
Family

Cutting Ties with
TOXIC FAMILY MEMBERS
and Loving Yourself
in the Aftermath

Dr. Sherrie Campbell

NEW YORK

LONDON • NASHVILLE • MELBOURNE • VANCOUVER

But It's Your Family
Cutting Ties with TOXIC FAMILY MEMBERS
and Loving Yourself in the Aftermath

Published in New York, New York, by Morgan James Publishing. Morgan James is a trademark of Morgan James, LLC. www.MorganJamesPublishing.com

Unless indicated otherwise, Scripture quotations are taken from the King James Version of the Bible. Public domain. Scripture quotations marked NASB are taken from the *New American Standard Bible*, © copyright 1960, 1962, 1963, 1968, 1971, 1972, 1973, 1975, 1977 by The Lockman Foundation. Used by permission.

ISBN 978-1-64279-099-3 paperback
ISBN 978-1-64279-100-6 eBook
Library of Congress Control Number: 2018905885

Cover Design by:
Rachel Lopez
www.r2cdesign.com

Interior Design by:
Bonnie Bushman
The Whole Caboodle Graphic Design

In an effort to support local communities, raise awareness and funds, Morgan James Publishing donates a percentage of all book sales for the life of each book to Habitat for Humanity Peninsula and Greater Williamsburg.

Get involved today! Visit
www.MorganJamesBuilds.com

To my daughter London—you are my Reason in life

Contents

Beneath the Surface

On the surface, it's confidence. It's strength.
It's resilience. It's focus. It's independence.
It's determination. It's power.
But beneath that same surface, there's just a little girl.
A little girl who has had to learn how to fight.
How to overcome. How to push through the pain. How to never give in.
How to never give up.
Beneath that same surface, there's just a little girl.
A little girl who has had to learn to get back up after every time she's fallen.
Who's had to learn that life is all hustle and no handouts.
On the surface, it's beauty. It's elegance. It's class. And it looks so easy.
So simple. So flawless.
But beneath that same surface is a story that most will never know.[1]

I am that little girl.

I am the family scapegoat.

Toxic family dynamics are a heart-centered topic for me—something I've done a tremendous amount of research and reading on to help me navigate through the healing of my own life. Here I want to share with you what I've learned along the way. In my first book, *Success Equations*, one of the life lessons I talk about is how important it is to share what we have learned with others. In *But It's Your Family*, I'm applying this life lesson toward you and toxic family dynamics. Whether you are a survivor of such a destructive upbringing or you care for someone who is, I pass along what follows to show that such a family life need not be the end of the matter but a critically important beginning. A beginning that leads into a much better life.

I weave threads of my story as well as stories of many of my patients and friends throughout this book to validate and further prove the research I present. As wonderful and validating as the research has been for my own healing, I am a believer that life's greatest teacher is always experience. I haven't just studied the psychological patterns and family dynamics behind the concepts. I have lived deeply in the mires of them my entire life. The mission I have is to help educate, identify, and bring clarity, closure, and healing to those of us who need this particular kind of information in order to move on and establish personal peace and happiness.

As a clinical psychologist, I am convinced that the one and only place authentic healing can take place is from the truth of our reality, no matter how ugly it may be.

Family may seem like a simple concept to many, but more than anything it's a concept heavily loaded and without a simple definition. In its most simple terms, the definition of *family* is one of a legal or genetic bond that exists between people. Yet, for many people, *family* means much more than that. Family is the place where "home" is. In this case, home is the originating place of unconditional love and support. If our family was healthy and we had a bad day, we couldn't wait to get home to take respite in the love and comfort we received in our home and from what our family members had to offer us.

Healthy families provide its members with an emotional and spiritual bond through the sharing of similar values, beliefs, traditions, shared experiences, and activities. Healthy families offer its members unconditional and nonjudgmental love and support. Family members feel surrounded by people who care about who they are and how they feel, and they each take an invested interest in helping each other grow into human beings who feel hopeful and positive toward self, others, and life as a whole. The dream common to all children is to have two parents who love them, who will be there to witness their most amazing accomplishments, to celebrate with them, and support them when they are down or when they have failed in one way or another. Healthy families provide all this and more.

On the other hand, for those of us who were raised in toxic family systems, the concept of *home* is quite different. Home equates to the creation of fear, anxiety, a lack of acceptance, and a lack of unconditional love and support. Home was the place we least wanted to be. Growing up in a toxic family is a hollow, confusing, maddening, and lonely experience. When we are raised by toxic parents, we live in a unique kind of crazy where we feel more like things to manage and keep on a schedule rather than as human beings to love, nurture, and care for. We leave childhood feeling emotionally homeless. Having a healthy home and family life is the dream we never got to experience growing up. We may have even glanced into the windows of other homes and felt envy for what we never had.

The most challenging aspect of psychological/emotional abuse is that is deniable by our family members and impossible to prove. Our family members don't believe they are abusing us because, by definition, they view themselves as perfect, and perfect people don't do imperfect things, such as emotionally manipulate their children. We as their children don't realize we're being manipulated because we believe the lies our toxic family members tell us, convinced everything is our fault and that we are the ones who are broken and destroying our family members.

Toxic family abuse is always two-fold. The first layer of abuse is the original poor treatment by our toxic family members, namely our parents. The second layer is their denial of the ways in which they treat and harm us, irrespective of the evidence as it manifests in our behavior and in our tragically low levels of self-worth. The sinister and obscure nature of their emotional abuse leaves us alone to pick up the crushed pieces of our self-worth and all aspects of how we function in life, love, and relationships. When we try and explain our fears of love, life, and people to others, we tend to come off sounding needy, desperate, and paranoid. This is because psychological abuse is not equipped with a clear set of descriptive indicators that our toxic family members find undeniably true. Consequently, to them at least, we can rarely if ever prove what has happened to us. All of the descriptors are subjective and therefore debatable, just as our toxic family members need for them to be. Because emotional abuse is impossible to prove, we often have an incredibly difficult time describing or putting into words what exactly has happened to us that is so bad. We know things were not or are not normal, but we don't know why. Emotional abuse moves quickly. Just as we're about to put our finger on it, it seems to slip away. Without a clear set of concrete, provable terms, many of us question if our abuse or neglect was real. Did it really happen? Or are we just making it up? We reason that if we were truly abused, our abuse should be easy to explain.

To add to our challenge of validating our experience, the average person isn't typically well educated or aware of emotional abuse, even when it is happening directly to him or her. Unless we have done the work to educate ourselves on emotional abuse, we cannot and will not be able to explain our situation. This allows the abusive treatment of our toxic family members to continue without interruption. Our toxic family members are experts at concealing their abusive behaviors just slightly under public radar so that when we complain about the hurt they have made us feel, our complaints fall on deaf ears. This level of slyness allows our toxic family members to walk away looking innocent and unfairly accused while we appear emotionally unstable. This is the most infuriating part for us.

It is important to understand that loving someone doesn't always mean having a relationship with that person, just like forgiveness doesn't always mean reconciliation. Reconciling, in many cases, only sets us up for more abuse. A significant part of our healing will come in accepting that not reconciling with certain people is a part of life. There are some relationships that are so poisonous that they destroy our ability to be healthy and to function at our best. When we put closure to these relationships, we give ourselves the space to love our toxic family members from a distance as fellow human beings where we do not wish harm upon them; we simply have the knowledge and experience to know it is unwise to remain connected with them.

My goal in what follows is to define what toxic is and present workable ideas and procedures we can all use to protect ourselves from toxic family abuse. When it comes to recovering from toxic family abuse, the first step that needs to happen is self-protection. Until that is in place, recovery or treatment cannot happen. Recovery and treatment center around the life-long journey of undoing the severe damage that destroyed our self-worth. Recovery entails learning to think, live, and love in healthy ways, with healthy boundaries, and with our own intuitive sense of what is right and what is wrong.

So welcome to the journey. It's a difficult one, perhaps harder than anything you've ever done. But it is also filled with hope—real, achievable hope. The kind of hope that brings genuine recovery and healing.

1

The Maddening World
of Manipulation

Toxic people. Who are they?

Is everyone toxic? No, not everyone is. That's the good news.

Can toxic people be our family members? Yes, they absolutely can. And that's the bad news.

Toxic can apply to our mother, father, siblings, grandparents, other extended family members, and even our own children.

None of us is perfect, that's for sure. We all have our flaws, but having flaws and being pathological or toxic are vastly different. Toxic people are hard to differentiate from other people because their toxicity isn't easy to discern to the ordinary observer, and this includes us as their family members. We assume that if our toxic family members appear good, they must be good. But that assumption is false. Appearances can betray the reality of what lies underneath, below the surface, out of the public eye. Toxic, in fact, is an *internal* state—the condition of a person's true character, mind-set, and will. And it can only be witnessed through the consistency and persistency of manipulative behavior.

When we're flawed, we have no problem owning up to our personal and relational foibles. We are able to laugh at ourselves when we make mistakes, and are more than willing to admit wrong and apologize whenever necessary. We seek peace, connection, clarity, and our own development rather than conflict.

People with pathological personalities, on the other hand, respond more like regressed, stubborn, vengeful bullies. They are never wrong. They are above apologies. They never question if they could have or should have done anything differently. And everything in their lives is an embellished drama of how they have been victimized by others.

With healthy persons, we are dealing with individuals who operate with a sense of balance and composure. They are self-reflective, logical, collected, and able to listen to others with an openness to learn.

But with a pathological person, we are dealing with the emotional immaturity of a two-to five-year-old in the body of an adult. The very reason toxic people are so frustrating to deal with is because we're looking at an adult but dealing with a toddler. The majority of us grew out of our two-year-old narcissism as a function of normal development. When an adult still responds from this regressed level of self-centeredness, it is very difficult for the visual and auditory parts of our brain to put a toddler's emotional response system inside of what looks and sounds like an adult, let alone when this adult is our parent. Like toddlers, toxic people base all their decisions on what they feel rather than on what is right. The thought of any consequences of their actions pale in comparison to getting what they want in the moment. Contrast this with healthy people: they think before they act and are mindful of how what they do may negatively impact themselves or others.

Toxic people cannot tolerate consideration of others. When trying to have a conversation with them, they are self-referential rather than self-reflective. When you share something about yourself with such people, they immediately turn the account into a story about them. The self-referential side of toxicity turns toxic people into the greatest one-uppers, name-droppers, and liars you'll ever come across. You cannot have a mutually beneficial conversation, where there is a natural back-and-forth flow. Sharing does not exist when communicating with toxic people. Of course, healthy flawed people sometimes do some of the same things that toxic people do. The difference, however, between ordinary and toxic lies is in the subtleness, persistence, and consistency of a toxic person's behaviors.

Healing Moment

There is very little randomness in the ways toxic people manipulate us. The wrongdoings they commit against us are perpetrated with the sole intention of draining us dry physically, emotionally, mentally, and spiritually.

Different Flavors of Toxic People

Toxic people come in all flavors. There are those who are *overtly* toxic and easy to spot (which makes them somewhat easier to deal with). This was my father. He is the classic Jekyll-and-Hyde personality. One minute he's loving and the next he's emotionally violent. Whenever we confront an overtly abusive person, he or she will tell us we deserved what we got.

Covertly toxic people aren't nearly as obvious, and therefore they are more baffling to deal with. Covert psychological abuse is sly, conniving, and confusing, making it extremely hard to spot and to know *for sure* if we are causing the problem or if it is truly the toxic person who is. My mother is this way. She is a passive-aggressive person who can say something that may on the surface appear benign but in reality is a dig into a core wound or sensitivity of mine that she created. I can best compare my mother to the character Mother Gothel in the movie *Tangled*. She abducted Rapunzel when she was a baby. In one scene, Mother Gothel and Rapunzel are standing in front of a full-length mirror. Mother Gothel says, "Rapunzel, look in that mirror. You know what I see? I see a strong, confident, beautiful young lady." She then looks over at Rapunzel and says, "Oh look, you're here too." Upon seeing the confused and hurt look on Rapunzel's face, Mother Gothel quickly retorts, saying with a sweet laugh, a finger bop on Rapunzel's nose, and an innocent smile on her face, "Oh, I'm just teasing. Stop taking everything so seriously."

When people are covertly toxic, they are masters at feigning innocence, of playing the victim, pretending to be less fortunate than others, and claiming that life has treated everyone better than it has treated them. Their emotional abuse is done in a secretive, undetectable manner where it's impossible to notice what's happening until it's too late. Anytime we try and confront covertly toxic family members, they are utterly appalled we would ever think they could do any of the things we're questioning them about. They immediately insinuate that we're the crazy ones. This is what Mother Gothel does to Rapunzel throughout the movie.

Shannon Thomas, author of *Healing from Hidden Abuse*, teaches that covert psychological abuse is similar to putting clear toxins in a glass of water. Once we drink the water, we cannot see the injury wreaking havoc inside of our body until our body starts reacting to the continued exposure to the poison. This is just how it happens with emotional abuse. The abuse is so covert and well hidden that we cannot immediately identify our emotional injuries. So we justify them and move on until it's too late and the poison has already created a deep wound in our psyche. As our relationships deepen with our toxic family members, so does their ability to manipulate us. If we are their children, their abuse started on our first day of life and will only deepen as we age or for as long as we remain connected to them.

Healing Moment

Deflecting their cruel actions onto their children is a favored manipulation tactic used by toxic family members.

Our toxic family members have a strong, impenetrable repulsion toward having to take responsibility for their actions. Scott Peck, psychiatrist and author of *The Road Less Traveled*, states that the majority of healthy people assume too much responsibility for the wrongs in their lives because they want to be the first to own their mistakes when it is necessary, whereas a toxic person won't take enough responsibility. Peck explains that when healthy persons are in conflict with the world, they automatically assume that *they* are at fault, but when toxic people are in conflict with the world, they automatically assume *the world* to be at fault. This is why our toxic family members are impossible to penetrate when we confront them about what they have done to us. They simply do not see themselves as the source of their problems. They see the world or us as the source of their troubles. So they fail to recognize their need for change.

Scott Peck also explains that healthy people who desire to take responsibility for their lives are said to drive themselves crazy while toxic people drive everyone else crazy. This could not be more true. Having been raised in a toxic family and watching myself attract one toxic person after another into my life and now treating patients in my office and thousands on Facebook (**www.facebook.com/sherriecampbellphd**), I have come to realize that toxic people will never take accountability for their actions. This is just the way it is with them, and it is this that is the missing piece that drives us all crazy. Accepting accountability for one's actions is what a healthy person does to help resolve a problem. This is an easy fix in the mind of someone who's healthy. But in a toxic person, this fix is out of the question. A toxic person is never at fault—or so he or she thinks. Therefore, accepting responsibility is not an option.

Here are some of the common traits of toxic people. See if any of these are present in the people you know, especially in those individuals who are closest to you.

- Nothing you can say or do is enough
- Believe they are perfect and never wrong
- Have to be the center of attention
- Ignore or engulf
- Rewrite history
- Invalidate you
- Rage at you
- Conflicts never get resolved
- Ruin special days and events
- Love your tragedies
- Separate and drive wedges between you and other family members
- Rigid and single-minded

- Low frustration tolerance, quick-tempered
- Little respect for differences
- Egocentric
- Self-preoccupied or self-involved
- Love their illnesses or injuries
- Comment on the smallest flaws or perceived imperfections
- Drag up your past and use it to hurt or embarrass you
- Leave you feeling guilty and ashamed of who you are
- Leave you feeling beaten, wounded, battered, bruised, and torn
- Violate your boundaries and never respect no as a response
- Show no empathy
- Do not care about your feelings and like to see you suffer
- Believe they are innocent and become offended at any evidence to the contrary

Notice that none of the traits of toxic people have anything to do with love. All of these traits are based in immaturity, selfishness, and manipulation, which is why being raised in toxic families is so confusing, empty, and painful.

Healthy people value consistency, predictability, connection, and communication when it comes to loving self and others. They feel horrible if they have inadvertently hurt another person, and they are willing to do whatever it takes to fix things.

Unhealthy people, on the other hand, are impossible to predict. There is always something hidden going on behind their back, there is no consistency in who they are from one moment to the next, and their actions rarely match the grandiosity of their words. They are word-magicians who pride themselves on being in control and unaffected by the needs of others.

People who are genuinely good-hearted will be kind to everyone, not just to the individuals from whom they stand to gain something. Genuine persons are not built on a set of false pretenses where they change personalities as a way to get what they want.

If you are living in constant confusion and feel as if your relationship with someone boils down to a delicate egg-shell walk, you are not in a relationship with a healthy person. You need to make some serious changes.

Healing Moment

 Love and drama cannot coexist.

The one thing that all the traits listed above have in common is selfishness. When we are with toxic family members, we will find that the entire trajectory of our life has to be, without choice or flexibility, all about their schedule, their needs, their feelings, their goals, their ideas, their illnesses … their *everything*. They are so controlling that before we even realize it, we are frantically living our life around their every whim and need because, if we don't, the consequences for us are disastrous. Toxic people cannot fathom that other people have needs of their own.

Being around my mother for five minutes is enough to wear me out. Within that short time, she's making the world all about her—her "hypoglycemia" or some other fictitious illness or injury of hers, and how these needs of hers have to control my schedule and dominate my life. She thinks of no one else but herself. Life functions around when she wakes up, when she eats, what she eats, being rigidly on time, what time she goes to bed, and how hard her mattress is. Even when we stay strictly on her schedule, she complains throughout the day that she's not on schedule. It's absolutely maddening. And on top of her overtly controlling nature, she gets frustrated with me for getting frustrated with her demand arsenal. If we get off her time schedule by even five minutes, she starts manifesting physical symptoms that have to be taken care of "right now" or else. Yet, she can travel across the country to different time zones and adjust, but the one-hour time difference for her to my home isn't doable.

It's these hypocrisies that tell me my mother's unreasonable and childish demands are manipulations she uses to become the center of everyone's focus.

She is at the controls, dictating how and when we all do anything, and all of this is based on her "needs" and demands. I have learned, as have many others, that there is no amount of bending, flexing, or being perfect we or anyone else can do that will ever be enough for these types of people. The more we give, the more we try, the more the toxic person in our life discredits our efforts and demands more. Toxic people operate more like a funnel than a waterproof bucket. Whatever we give seems to go right through them rather than filling any part of them for more than a few minutes. Their behavior and expectations are absolutely mind-boggling. Before we know it, we are left exasperated, exhausted, defeated, and frustrated beyond belief, with no hope that anything about who we are or will ever be will ever be enough. Then, to top off the situation, they accuse us of being selfish when all we have done is tried to meet their incessant, irrational, and self-centered demands. This is the maddening world of manipulation that toxic people create.

Healing Moment

 We must examine how our toxic family members make us feel and begin to consider the idea of when enough is enough.

What Is Healthy Love?

Our toxic family members insist that they love us. But if they are unhealthy, then whatever they believe about love must be unhealthy too. What, then, is *healthy* love?

Sadly, a large majority of us are more experienced with unhealthy love than with having any idea or clue about what healthy love is or even looks like. Many of us question if we would recognize healthy love if it hit us square in the face, and if it did, would we like it? This is especially true for those of us who were raised in toxic family environments. When we start life without knowing healthy love—including what it is, what it looks like, and what it feels like—we find it incredibly challenging to find healthy love later in life. After all, we don't even know what we are looking for.

The first place to start when trying to determine if what we have is healthy love is to look at how we feel around someone the majority of the time we are with him or her. If we feel consistent anxiety, a lack of trust, paranoia, like we're walking on eggshells, that we can't be ourselves, and feeling as if we would rather avoid talking so as to avoid arguing, we are not in a healthy love dynamic.

Healthy love happens when two givers come together. When this happens, it's like magic. It becomes a connection of *you nurture me and I will nurture you and together we will grow*. Healthy love is fun and lighthearted. Can you imagine it? This is what we all deserve: to have our hearts held as something deeply precious in the hands of those who raised us.

When we are brought up in toxic families, healthy love is hard to fathom, but it is available and achievable. We just have to know how to find it and how to create it in our own lives. Here are some clues regarding what to look for when looking for love:

- When love is present, there is very little chaos.
- When love is present, there is conversation.
- When love is present, there is no gossip or backstabbing.
- When love is present, there is support and nurturing.
- When love is present, there is acceptance.
- When love is present, there is ease and room for joy.
- When love is present, there is clarity.
- When love is present, we feel stable.
- When love is present, we can be ourselves.
- When love is present, we are not consumed with worry.
- When love is present, we have a sense of community.
- When love is present, we feel happy.
- When love is present, we live in a state of trust.
- When love is present, we experience contentment.

Do Toxic People Know What They're Doing?

Because we love our family members and want desperately for them to love us back, we choose to believe they don't mean to treat us the way they do. When we rationalize and justify their mistreatment of us, it is called *reverse projection*. Bree Bonchay, author of *I Am Free*, explains that we relate to our toxic family members as if they are normal healthy people who possess a conscience, self-awareness, and a sense of integrity. Because of this inherent trust in them, we believe their words. We know that we don't lie or manipulate so we believe our toxic family members would never lie to or manipulate us. We give them the benefit of the doubt because we believe they genuinely love us. Because we believe they truly love us, we cannot believe they could ever or would ever do anything to intentionally hurt us. When we believe in this way, we are essentially projecting our own good qualities or character traits onto the toxic family members we love. So when they don't respond in the ways that a loving, kind, healthy person would, we are left feeling hurt and confused and questioning ourselves, believing we must somehow be to blame for their lack of love and understanding.

Healing Moment

Toxic people do not think, operate, or play by the same rules we do, and our failing to recognize this sets us up by default for manipulation and unhappiness.

Reverse projection keeps us in a place of denial and with the problem in our hands. As long as we believe we are the problem, we hold the false belief that we can fix or solve the problem. If we can change ourselves to be better, we believe we will have the power to fix things.

But consider this: if we are not the problem and the real problem actually is our toxic family members, then we have no shot at changing the dynamic.

Moreover, the reality is that we cannot change anyone but ourselves. Once I came to this realization in my own therapy, I felt a deep sense of sadness before I felt any relief. It felt hopeless to me when the problem wasn't in my hands or my responsibility to fix. I had to start the process of grieving the loss of my hope—the hope that kept me going back again and again for my family's "love."

And that's what I never received even though I worked so hard for it. I was continually discarded.

Best-selling author Shahida Arabi says to the claim that our toxic family members don't know what they're doing or that they don't know any better is completely false. She says that "anyone who has the intellectual capacity to blame-shift, gaslight, project and stage a smear campaign to escape accountability has the intellectual capacity to be aware of their own blame and to process it when the victim says 'this hurts'."[2]

Healing Moment

 Our toxic family members know what they're doing, but they don't care about what they're doing. The reason they don't care is because what they do works for them so they see no reason to do things differently.

H. G. Tudor, in his remarkable and eye-opening book *Manipulated*, teaches that toxic people do not care about the results of their actions because they are driven by an all-consuming need for fuel. This need for them is so overwhelming that any consideration of the results of their actions falls a distant second to their need to secure their fuel. Our toxic family members leave behind a legacy of pain, chaos, and confusion. They want our focus to be on them at all times. They crave, need, and want this attention. Without our emotional reactions, our fears, or our tears, or without us pouring our love and neediness all over them, they cannot experience their own existence.

So what is their fuel? Tudor sums it up in two simple concepts: emotional reaction and attention.

How do our toxic family members secure our emotional reactions and consume our attention? Manipulation.

Our toxic family members may believe inside themselves that they love us, but ultimately, they live through us to use us. They feed off of having the power and authority to manipulate, degrade, and create insecurity, fear, sadness, neediness, guilt, feelings of obligation, hope, and rage in us. This is their fuel. This is what they live on. They use us to keep themselves going.

When I was growing up, my mother made me feel emotions I can only describe as fury. The feeling I felt inside was beyond anger, frustration, or annoyance; it was pure, unadulterated fury. I felt like there was an emotional tsunami swirling inside of me, but I couldn't pinpoint the exact reason why. What I didn't know at that time were all the subtle ways in which she was passive-aggressively baiting me to rage. Once I would get to that point, she would then accuse me of being the abuser and claim her role as the victim. All I ever felt growing up under her was head-spun.

Healing Moment

 A toxic parent will provoke an independent child to anger in order to feel superior and to "prove" the child's flaws.[3]

—*Shannon Thomas*

It's Not about Love or Hate

Here's the reality, the truth of the matter: Our toxic family members don't love. They don't hate either. These emotions are too deep and too genuine and require too much authenticity, time, depth, energy, and commitment for toxic people. My therapist explained to me that my parents *do feel*, but they feel solely for themselves. They are egocentric, and they do not, cannot, and will not feel for me or for the things they have done to me. They will only focus on my reaction to their abuse and how my reaction made *them* feel. The only thing our toxic family members process is if they feel loved or hated, regardless of what they've done to cause and provoke our negative or positive reactions. Who we are and what we feel are not considerations for them. In some way it's not always that our toxic family members are *trying* to hurt us; rather, they just aren't thinking about us at all, which is almost worse.

Our toxic family members may tell us they love or hate us, but they only do so to provoke a strong reaction out of us. When we're loving them, it's a sweet and potent experience for them, but they will get bored with that so they will switch things up. Out of what seems like nowhere to us, they will become those hateful, cruel, discarding, schoolyard bullies who ignore us, gossip about us, smear us, and make us feel as if we are the worst people on earth. This puts us into a state of intense confusion. Our toxic members feed off watching us feel confused, angry, and frustrated as we try and reason with them. This is exactly the kind of attention and emotional reaction they seek. They enjoy watching us scramble to understand their abusive behavior and all the work and effort we put forth trying to get them to take responsibility for how they've treated us. It's all of our scrambling that makes them *feel*. They don't deeply consider loving us or hating us. They only think about manipulating us. They love pulling us in close and making us feel safe so they can enjoy the thrill of throwing us out, without warning, the minute they feel they have secured our love. What they "love" is watching us lose ourselves. They "love" knowing they have that kind of control over us.

Healing Moment

 Power is a toxic person's drug.

Can They Be Treated with Medication or Psychotherapy?

I can say from personal experience, not only in my personal life but also in the nearly thirty years of clinical training and experience I've had, that toxic people are largely untreatable. Here's why.

Medication doesn't work because being toxic is not a brain chemistry issue but a character defect. Medications, such as mood stabilizers, may tame a toxic person's moodiness, but these medications do not impact the flaws in their character. I have witnessed the toxic people in my office do just fine in therapy as long as all the fault for their problems are placed upon another person, including on their children or their spouse. The minute the therapy starts to turn on them and their character flaws, toxic people almost always quit therapy. They leave feeling victimized because therapy was "too hard," or they leave threatening to take "legal action" with no legal or ethical reasons to do so. I have yet to experience a toxic person who hasn't become invasive to my life outside of therapy with emails or voicemails demanding the ways in which he or she thinks I should be doing my job.

Scott Peck lets us know that the more toxic individuals are, the more dishonest they are in their behavior and the more distorted they are in their thinking. This doesn't allow us, as clinicians, to help them because they do not have any insight. A vampire is a fictional character who cannot see their reflection in a mirror. Toxic people are like this in that they cannot see within themselves. They lack insight. The psychological definition of *insight* is:

- The capacity to show understanding for one's own or another's mental processes;
- The immediate understanding of the significance of an event or action;
- The ability to understand one's own problems.

In my therapy practice, I find that I invariably treat healthy people who come in to learn how to deal and cope with the toxic people in their lives, thereby leaving the real patient untreated. Toxic people live lives of pure falsehood, which leaves us as clinicians feeling confused, repulsed, irritated, and completely overwhelmed by their arsenal of twisted motives, victimology, incessant one-sided views, pitiful tears, and inaccurate communications where everything is either blamed on us or on others. Peck explains that when clinicians begin to feel revulsion around their toxic patients, this, more than anything else, is the red flag that clinicians are in the presence of evil persons. Revulsion is a powerful emotion that causes us to immediately want to avoid or escape being around this type of toxic individual. We begin to feel overcome by our own feelings of dread at the thought of treating them because of their flagrant, consistent, and persistent defiant refusal to look at the truth, and their rejection of any offers for help and to any ideas outside of their own; subsequently, these patients do not last in a therapy office.

Toxic people will do nearly anything to avoid the emotional pain that comes along with self-examination. They loath any process that puts them under the kind of analysis that could expose their deceptive ways. More research needs to be done on such personality disorders to find effective ways to treat them. We are not there yet. We can have compassion for such toxic individuals, but at this point there is no clear or effective way to treat them. It doesn't help the clinician that toxic people see nothing wrong with who they are or the mass of destruction they leave in their wake. They have no interest in changing and do not appear to suffer from or recognize their low self-worth, which is exactly what allows them to continue being the cruel people they are. The more they harden their heart to the malicious and cruel ways they treat others, the more heartless and free they feel to continue operating in their abusive ways.

In his book *People of the Lie*, Scott Peck describes toxic as evil. He teaches that "Evil is that force, residing either inside or outside of human beings that seeks to kill life and liveliness. ... Evil has nothing to do with natural death; it is concerned only with unnatural death, with the murder of the body or the spirit."[4] Toxic people spread destruction and death to those who come in contact with them. The closer we get to them, the more we will experience their deadly poison. We have no cure for them that they will accept. The best we can do is find a remedy for the damage they have done to us.

Lyric Therapy
I know I am enough, possible to be loved
It was not about me
Now I have to rise above
Let the universe call the bluff
Yeah, the truth will set you free
—"By The Grace of God," by Katy Perry[5]

2

Toxic Parents

When it comes to the toxic family system, the poison is always on the inside, deep in the core of the family. The core is nearly always the parents. Whether overtly or covertly, the poison (the way our parents manipulate us) is the family secret no one on the inside is allowed to expose or talk about. On the outside, our parents may appear to be healthy, likable people, but that's only a smoke screen they have delicately set in place. They excel at and thrive on deception. Every member of the family is expected to follow suit. For our toxic family members, the image they present of our family is of the utmost importance to them, which is why deception dominates the system; the image presented is false.

When we are raised in this dynamic, it is too easy to think there is something wrong with us. We somehow know that any moment of rebellion against this system—standing up to it or exposing it—will be met with a fierce twisting of the truth. We will be blamed for being the mean, abusive, and emotionally unstable persons in the family. For this reason, we often feel like we have to over-explain and justify the reasons we need to protect ourselves, our children, and our lives from our family's emotional abuse and manipulation of others.

Healing Moment

 There is no life in this type of dynamic.

Danu Morrigan, author of *You're Not Crazy—It's Your Mother*, says there are two types of toxic parents: the Ignoring Parent and the Enmeshed Parent. The Ignoring Parent will show very little interest in us, and some in this group will ignore us to the point of neglect. My ex-husband is this way with my daughter. He, at almost fifty years old, doesn't own a place or even have an apartment to live in. He rents a room in either a friend's place or a stranger's home, even when he has the available income to, at the very least, rent a two-bedroom apartment. He prefers to spend his money on video games and other frivolous things that make him happy than to provide an appropriate lifestyle for his daughter. He ignores all the signs and signals that our daughter wants to spend the least amount of time with him as possible.

When she is there with him, she doesn't have her own space, and he plays computer games or watches sports all day yelling at the TV while ignoring her needs. He pays very little child support, doesn't plan anything special for their time together, takes her to Starbucks on dinner nights to play his video games while she does homework, and chooses to live over an hour away from where her life is. He tells himself every lie he needs to about who he is as a parent and the imagined closeness of their relationship to convince himself he's a highly involved good parent. Because our daughter is successful, he takes credit for parenting her, even though he has less than 5 percent shared custody. As her custodial time with me has increased over the years due to his inability to live a responsible life, he has never offered to pay more child support to help fund her needs.

Enmeshed Parents, on the other hand, view themselves as symbiotic with their children. They see their children as extensions of who they are, and therefore try to dictate their children's lives—their choices—providing them no freedom to separate and individuate into healthy, unique, self-sufficient, confident people. Enmeshed Parents have clear expectations for their child's success, popularity, and image, and they give their children an opinion about everything, from what they wear, who they date, and what they eat to the college they should attend, the career path they should take, and even their marital and family-planning decisions. Such parents will undermine our parenting rules or methods of discipline when we have our own children, thereby ensuring that their emotional manipulation continues into the next generation. Danu Morrigan shows that it is much harder to remove ourselves from an enmeshed parent than it is to remove ourselves from an ignoring parent because when we're enmeshed—when what's happening to us is just always the way things have been—we don't realize how deeply trapped we are.

Selfishness and Parenting

Psychologically immature parents are too self-consumed to suffer with their children. They prefer to *cause* suffering to their children as a way to feel powerful, important, needed, in control, and not the problem. Peck states in his book *The Road Less Traveled* that children feel if their parents are willing to suffer with them, they will tell themselves "then suffering must not be so bad," and they will become more willing to suffer when on their own. In other words, children come to trust that there is nothing unsafe or wrong with them when they are suffering. In order for parents to be present to and suffer with their children, their children need three simple things from them: *time*, *love*, and *attention*. Toxic parents provide none of these things, certainly not in any healthy ways.

Healing Moment

 The quality of time our parents devote to us indicates the degree to which we believe we are valued.

As a child, I hardly had any quality time with either of my parents. My father was hardly ever around as he skipped the state many times to avoid paying child support and lived away from us more than he ever lived near us. My mother was always busy with her own life. Work is where she garnered her identity, and because of this, she put work above all else, including above her marriages. She had little time left over for her husbands or her children. Further, she went to bed so early that her husbands and children rarely had quality time with her. I appreciate that she provided for us, and I am clear that her career was more for her benefit than ours. My mother ran a rigid schedule for us as children based largely on her needs to eat at the time that worked best for her to make sure she could get to bed early. With her time, her flexibility was little to none, unless it involved something she wanted to do for herself. I have no memory of mother-daughter days like I share with my daughter. I had two vacations with my mom when I was in my early twenties, but only because she didn't have a man to go with her.

The majority of toxic parents fail to assume even an adequate or healthy sense of responsibility for their parenting. They brush their children off in a million different ways in lieu of providing them with the necessary time, love, and attention their children need to develop into whole, confident people.

On the other extreme, some toxic parents enmesh their children, demanding to know every gory detail of their lives, and these parents live their lives nearly stalking their child's every move, adding doses of guilt if their child isn't with them all the time. Toxic parents absolutely lack the empathy necessary to put anyone's needs above their own. When children are shown a lack of empathy or understanding by their parents, they turn into depressed, angry, and somewhat lifeless children. Toxic parents see zero problem with meeting their own needs before ours, and they feel 100 percent justified in doing so. Toxic parents create deep and justifiable resentments within us as children and then act clueless as to why they have no authentic relationship with us as adults.

Many parents who veer on the side of being unloving conceal their true nature by making frequent professions of love to us or about us. These professions were repetitive and mechanical as they told us and others how loved we were and how proud they were of us. In reality, however, they did not devote any significant quality time with us. As children, we were never fulfilled by their empty words, even though we may have consciously clung to them, wanting to believe the words they said. But deep down we know what our parents did rarely reflected what they said.

Healing Moment

 Selfishness and parenting cannot coexist.[6]

The Development of Personal Value

Parents are responsible for the development of our personal value. Peck shares a basic law of child development: "Wherever there is a major deficit in parental love, the child will, in all likelihood, respond to the deficit by assuming itself to be the cause of the deficit, thereby developing an unrealistically negative self-image."[7] If we start life with a deep sense of self-doubt due to poor parenting, we either become underachievers or overachievers. If we are the overachiever, which I am, we achieve in some way under the guise that, *if I achieve enough, then maybe I will become important to my parents; maybe they will see me and validate my worth.* I can say in my case, not my brother's, that the more I have succeeded, the more my parents have loathed me. Yet, I have heard both of my parents say, "I must have done something right because you and your brother are both successful." It's surreal to me that instead of seeing our accomplishments for what they are—ways to secure their love or establish our independence from them—they take personal parenting credit for our accomplishments.

Peck teaches that the feeling of being valued—"I am a valuable person"— is essential to the development of our self-worth and is the cornerstone of what makes us successful throughout life. If we start life with a deep sense of our value, we are a step ahead of the game.

I don't have parents who are genuinely proud of me, and I know this by how they treat me. How about you? Do your parents genuinely value you?

When we grow up feeling of little value, that we are not worth caring for, we learn not to care for ourselves, and this is exactly what happened to me. Loving myself had to become my own mission. My first book, *Loving Yourself: The Mastery of Being Your Own Person*, was a huge step for me in starting my recovery. I was able to identify, organize, and conceptualize the problems I struggled with so deeply throughout my childhood. Unfortunately, I was naive to think this book could help heal my family. It was written from the innocent girl perspective. At that time in my life, I was full of hope, believing that if I told my story and my family read it, they would finally validate me as worthy and would naturally feel terrible for the mistakes they made and for how recklessly and neglectfully they treated me. I envisioned the "Oprah Moment" of us bonding and growing together from all I had shared with such openness and vulnerability. Envisioning them loving me, I wrote about how my parents did the best they could for who they were at the time they raised me. I offered them forgiveness throughout the book and was generous toward their mistakes.

My family knew I was writing this book. Prior to writing the self-help sections, my father read all the poetry. In fact, he said to me that if writing the book was going to help me heal in some way, he wanted me to write it. He was "over it," he said, meaning he had accepted who he was. Now he wanted me to heal myself.

My mother's dearest friend read the book after I had finished it and told my mother that what I had done in my life to heal myself was personal work she had regretfully never done herself and that my book was truly amazing.

My mother helped finance my book, but she refused to read it, telling me she "wouldn't be able to handle it." I supported her decision because I didn't want *her* to feel bad. Now I can see her decision for what it was—a complete refusal to take any real accountability for her parenting. My mother didn't want to feel ashamed of *herself*. She didn't have empathy for me or want to learn about my pain or do anything to help mend it. She handed that job over to my therapist and the family we were close to who suggested I be placed in therapy. My mother didn't want to face what I had written because it would hurt *her*. She didn't feel bad for *me*. She never has.

On my forty-second birthday, four months after *Loving Yourself* was released, my mother, father, and brother emotionally destroyed me for writing it.

On. My. Birthday!

My mother was with me in person for this birthday. Anytime I confronted her with a tear-soaked face, angrily and desperately pleading for her to see how abusive she was behaving, she would cryptically say, "Well, you must be right; you're the shrink." This time was no different. My daughter was there with me. I remember my daughter asking me if we would ever see my mother again. I told her that I did not know. I was so lost for words that "I don't know" is all I could choke out.

My brother, who I loved so much as a child, was the ringleader of my demise on that day. My last words to my brother via text were "I love you." His last word to me was "classic."

My father's last words to me over the phone were, "You make me look inept in this book. Just to be clear, had I assaulted you, I would have put your ass in the hospital."

I was beyond emotionally crushed. I was totally confused and caught off guard.

Why did you support me and pretend you were okay while the book was being written? They all knew the topic and content. They even contributed to its production. But all they really did was set me up to be destroyed after its release.

Their hypocrisy disgusted me, especially since the writing of the book was not a shock. They all knew about it—and for several years! Writing it took me seven years. My family had made me feel supported all the way through it. But their hostile reaction on my birthday deepened within me more than ever that there was no hope. I was not loved, and my parents did not ever do their best with me. I regret ever giving them the grace I did.

My dream for a healing with my family was over.

I would never receive anything close to an Oprah Moment.

I had no value to them as a child, and I had no value to them as an adult. That was my reality.

Why choose the birthday of the daughter you were supposed to love and care for only to intentionally and purposefully annihilate her? They had the months leading up to my birthday, and seven years prior to the publishing of my book. They could have spoken up or confronted me at any time during those months and years.

So why did they choose my birthday? It took me a while to figure this out, but now I know the answer. Because they *consciously* chose *that* day to crush me. They knew it would be the perfect time to cause me the worst amount of emotional pain, abandonment, and rejection.

I remember looking over at my mother that night. I was noticeably fighting back tears, and I saw her looking at me. The look she had on her face was nervous but cold. She showed no empathy. What I saw was only curiosity. She seemed to be wondering if she had finally pushed her cruelty too far with me. Had she finally destroyed her favorite cat toy? Sadly, it took me four more years to finally cut the cord with her.

I've learned that this is how toxic families operate. Some parents use emotional gang-up warfare and complete abandonment as tools for communication, manipulation, and punishment. When parents sacrifice love for their need for control and domination over their children, their reward is children who are excessively fearful for the future and doubt themselves.

Healing Moment

Toxic parents make their children deeply doubtful of their own lovability, significance, importance, and personal value in this world as a way to maintain manipulative control and to keep them from telling the family secrets.

The Goal of Toxic Family Systems

What has become clear to me over time is that genuine and loving connections are not the sought after or desired goal in toxic family systems. My parents thrived on the divide-and-conquer technique. My dad consistently and persistently spoke poorly about my mother, my brother, my brother's wife— in fact, whoever he saw as getting in the way of him being the center of attention. My mother made my dad the "bad guy," and whenever I stood up for myself or against her in any way, she would cryptically say, "You're just like your father." My mother talked poorly to me about everyone in my family behind their backs, and I've been in earshot when she's done the same to me.

In toxic families, siblings are often pitted against each other, which was also done in my case and continues to this day. This is how the scapegoat and golden child roles between siblings are created. The triangulation may be subtle or overt, but the damage to the relationships between siblings is fully accomplished. In my case, my brother and I were close as children because we had to survive together. At times he was the parent I never had, and at other times I filled that empathic parental role for him, especially when we were young adults. No matter the closeness we shared as children, he was still the worshiped golden child and I the scapegoat.

Growing up as the family scapegoat was deeply painful for me. I wanted more than anything to be loved in all the ways everyone loved my brother. I watched both parents bend the world on its axis to be part of my brother's athletic world, and I stood witness to the fact that my parents hardly did anything to be part of my world. My moments in life just weren't as bright as his. My brother wasn't just adored by my parents and most everyone else in the small town we grew up in. He was worshiped. I worshiped him too, yet still never felt jealous of him as a person. In fact, for years I viewed him as the only positive thing about me. I was related to him, and because he was good, I had at least one thing about me other people would like.

Why would any parent want to create separation and division among their family members, especially their children? They do this in order to maintain manipulative control over the relationship dynamics within the family. The effort is all about divide and conquer. If my brother wasn't giving my parents the attention and emotional validation they needed, they would elevate me to his status behind my back in an effort to make him insecure about losing his golden child status. This must have been painful and scary for my brother, and largely the reason he has wanted zero connection with me as an adult because, as a child, I was never the star. I was the "bad kid, the screw up." Who wants to be replaced by the loser kid? Not my brother.

I always lived in my brother's shadow and without bitterness. I absolutely adored him. I never had any desire to be better than him because I never even saw that as a possibility. After all, he was the family superhero, the kid my parents could most readily and narcissistically feast off of. All I wanted for myself was to find my own tiny sliver of sunlight to bask in. When I found this in my success, my parents bragged about it to my brother as a way to stifle his independence from them. This served to drive the wedge between my brother and me even deeper.

The family scapegoat becomes what therapists call the "identified patient," or IP. According to Virgina Satir, renowned family therapist and author, "Identified Patient is a term used in a clinical setting to describe the person in a dysfunctional family who has been subconsciously selected to act out the family's inner conflicts as a diversion; who is the split-off carrier of the family disturbance."[8] In other words, the scapegoat is the bad kid, the one who often suffers from eating disorders, poor grades, rebellion, poor attendance, illness, depression, and anger. Scapegoats are blamed for all the troubles in the family because their bad behavior is putting everyone else under so much stress.

Ultimately, as the scapegoat, we are the symptom bearers of the family, acting out all the family's dysfunction, and then our family members scapegoat us for it. Scott Peck shows that toxic parents have to have a scapegoat because, in their own hearts, they consider themselves above reproach, which causes them to lash out at anyone who criticizes them. More often than not, once the identified patient starts treatment, the clinician usually discovers that the source of the problem does not lie with the child but with the parents. The child is not found to be as sick as his or her parents. Although the parents have identified the child as the one in need of improvement, it is usually they, the identifiers, who need the treatment. The parents are the ones who should be the patients. Peck believes the most immediate need to be met for the identified patient is not treatment but protection—protection from toxic family members.

The worst thing that ever happened for my parents is that the family we were close to throughout my childhood suggested my mother put me in therapy. There has been, and continues to be, a very negative reaction to the improvements in my knowledge and mental health because, over time and through much self-examination, I have come to know the truth: I was not the problem; the parenting I received was the problem in my family dynamics; I was just a symptom of toxic parenting.

Danu Morrigan clarifies that being the scapegoat can actually be a sort of gift. The role actually helps the child much more in the long term than does the role of the golden child. The scapegoat is far more likely to question the family dynamics, to see how poisonous they are, to seek answers and help, and to eventually escape from the toxic family web. The golden child, however, hardly ever escapes. The golden child lives life completely enmeshed with his toxic parents doing all he can to secure their attention and keeping his role in making the family look good.

Healing Moment

Dysfunctional families despise the truth-tellers and whistle-blowers. They are all about admiring the Emperor's new clothes, and they turn on anyone who dares to mention the nakedness.[9]

—*Danu Morrigan*

All toxic families are different in how they run their destructive divide-and-conquer manipulative patterns. What follows are some of the ways toxic families achieve their aim of maintaining manipulative power.

Ostracize

Some parents require that the family silence one person as a way to show disapproval for who "we" are or how "we" are behaving. When one person is shunned, it is clear to that person that she is being disparaged and rejected. She receives the message that she doesn't belong and isn't good enough to be a part of the core group. The core group's purposeful cruelty creates deep shame in the outed person. Is there any greater pain than to feel like you don't belong to the group of people who are supposed to love you the most?

In-group/out-group

In my family, I was nearly always in the out-group unless my parents needed me when my brother wasn't giving them the attention they wanted. I never heard the end of it from my mother regarding her annoyance and hatred for her younger sister. Nor did I ever hear the end of her talking horribly about each man she married and the subsequent stepchildren she had to deal with. I never knew from day to day which of her friends were in the in-group or who was in the out-group for "bullying" her. My father behaved in all these same ways with his wives and friends. Through my own healing, I've come to see that the real bullies in each relationship dynamic were my parents.

Excessive gossip

Some families divide and conquer using gossip as the way to manipulate and create tension between people. My family was notorious for this. The overall aim of gossip used by our toxic parents is to break us, their children, down little by little over time. They strategically manipulate in this. It's the best way for them to keep us from questioning them and their actions while keeping us so deeply confused about what is going on that the only one we question is ourselves. They get us to question our own reasoning, our sanity, and our perceptions of reality. The more slowly and deeply they can keep us confused about who they are and questioning who we are, the more we gradually lose touch with our own sense of right and wrong. Problems are relentlessly blamed on whoever the identified patient is at the time. The more our toxic parents break us down, the less confidence we have to activate for ourselves because we've lost touch with the reality of who our toxic parent are—cruel and manipulative people.

Healing Moment

This kind of control is not hard for parents to get over their children. It's terrifying for children to see their parents as insufficient or flawed. Children only feel safe if they have parents they trust they can count on.

Toxic Cycle of Emotional Abuse

The cycle that emotional abuse takes in toxic families is a four-stage process:

- Idealize
- Devalue

- Discard
- Hoover

The first stage of the cycle is being *idealized*. When our toxic parents idealize us, everything feels great, even better than great. We get a taste of what it feels like to be safe, loved, and seen. We feel significant to our family members. It's as if we're living in the penthouse of the Tower of Love.

However, the idealized stage is the most short-lived, especially if we are the scapegoated child. Once our toxic family members feel certain we're feeling secure and trusting them, they immediately begin to subtly *devalue* us.

When we are being devalued, it is not obvious. Our toxic family members often start by subtly ignoring us or sending out passive-aggressive digs about how we're somehow annoying them or not measuring up. They make us feel as if we're in their way. These subtle rejections hurt us, but in this stage we're not sure if we're just overreacting or if the rejections are real. When our toxic family members see the confusion on our faces, they trick us by claiming they were just joking. But make no mistake. That joking is a cut down. And in our gut, we know they are revealing what they really think of us. We begin to feel insecure and afraid and often start trying to please our toxic family members in an effort to maintain feeling the security of their love and acceptance.

The more we please our toxic family members in this stage, the more annoyed they get and start accusing us of being too sensitive, insecure, or needy. They insinuate that nothing has changed and that we're reading too deeply into every little thing they say or do. The confusion we feel inside intensifies because their actions tell us an entirely different story, leaving us with no clarity and at war within ourselves. The more insecure we feel, the more desire we show to feel safe, the more ostracizing and rejecting our toxic family members become. They use our needy behavior as justification to completely *discard* us.

When we get emotionally discarded, we've been abandoned. We may still live in the same house with our toxic family members, but we are not feeling accepted or wanted. The worst thing for any human being to feel, especially a child, is undesirable and unwanted, like there is something so horrible about us that we don't deserve love. We usually experience being emotionally discarded by our toxic family members as an intense feeling of not fitting in with them, that we are not important, that we offer no value to their lives, and that whatever is so bad about us must be bad enough that our toxic family members don't even show a desire or interest to fix anything with us. Some of us may experience being discarded as a feeling that our existence means nothing to our toxic family. Any attempts on our part to talk to them about how we're feeling are met with them acting as if they have no clue what we're talking about, which leads us to question if we're losing our mind.

Healing Moment

 Being brushed aside is the easiest way to discard a child.

Once we hit bottom, abandoned and rejected, we somehow have to find a way to peel ourselves off the ground like a fruit roll-up. It is here, when we're at the very bottom, that glimmers of true hope begin to grow—not hope in our toxic family members, but hope in ourselves because we realize we are all we have. We start to process plan B. We begin to wonder if our toxic parents are unable to love us. Maybe there are other ways we can find a sense of security. When I was really young, I used to have fantasies that both my parents would die and that a loving family would see me feeling alone and dejected at their funeral and would want to adopt me. This was my plan B.

The pain that being discarded creates wakes us up a bit, and we begin to come to a new understanding about our toxic family members because we are alone now and have no other choice. When we're at the bottom, we often find a sense of our own anger through our despair and come to believe that we're being treated unfairly, that we must have rights, and that we deserve to be treated better. We start reading books and may even enter some type of therapy.

Just as our toxic family members sense we may actually be catching onto their abusive ways, they move into stage four of the abuse cycle. They begin doing all they can to suck us back in, the part of the cycle called *hoovering* (which will be discussed in detail in a later chapter). Our toxic parents and other family members entice us when we are the most wounded and are beginning to look at options to start to heal ourselves. They take this opportune time to pull us back in for some much-needed loving attention, and we are idealized once again—renewing the ongoing destructive cycle of emotional abuse.

Healing Moment

Emotional abuse and manipulation cannot work without moments of intermittent kindness.

Shannon Thomas explains that psychologically abusive people can only maintain normalcy for short spurts of time. Being an authentically caring, decent person isn't foundational for them. They must fake the emotions and behaviors that suggest their character is positive. Because their decent personality traits aren't real, our toxic family members quickly return to their normal state of affairs. Thomas validates that the hard swing back to our family's abusive ways is always more painful after a time of being idealized. These sparse moments of counterfeit kindness are powerful enough to rekindle our hope in the security and love we want from our family. This type of toxic family dynamic causes us to live in hope and in fear. We can easily become addicted to our feelings of hope, which lead us to relax and feel things are starting to turn for the better. But as soon as hope seems it might settle in, we find ourselves beaten up and discarded once again. The repeated and sneaky nature of this type of emotional dysfunction is exactly why breaking away from our toxic family members is so difficult.

Who doesn't want to be loved and treasured by their family? Who wakes up in the morning just hoping their family members will say and do horrible things to them? No one, not ever. Belonging is at the core of our human experience. We are hardwired to want and need to be included. Feelings of disconnection are at the very core of our sadness, our anger, and our feelings of not being accepted for who we are. Every one of us desires to feel we have a group of people who love and need us. It is this exact human necessity our toxic parents exploit in us for their gain.

The overall experience we have of our poisonous family is one that is deeply hurtful. Healing from toxic family dynamics is a slow journey. It takes time to do the personal work necessary to rewire our deeply held beliefs around the idea of who we are and the reality of who our family members are. When we're not aware of the abusive cycle we're in, each time we're idealized we instantly go back and forfeit the growth and learning we achieved and the anger we felt because being idealized again by our tribe feels so safe and so good that we convince ourselves that it's going to be different this time. I can tell you from personal experience and from treating people in my office that it is never different for long. Each and every time we're discarded and tossed from the Tower of Love, we incur even more emotional damage, and it takes us longer and longer to heal because our wounds continue to deepen and misshape us.

Lifelong Feelings of Emotional Loneliness

To feel emotionally lonely as a child is remarkably devastating. Lindsay Gibson, author of *Adult Children of Emotionally Immature Parents*, shows that emotional loneliness develops from not having experienced enough love and connection with others. In children, it develops from feeling invisible to their self-preoccupied parents. To add to our loneliness and confusion, our toxic parents often look and act normal, and they provide for our food, home, and shelter, but they do very little to connect or bond with us emotionally. Because of this, we leave our childhood with gaping holes where true security should have been. I have been told countless times by many people, "I just love your mom." I am sure they do. She often treated other people's children with more kindness than she showed me. But such positive comments made about my mother only served to make me feel even lonelier and crazier. If everyone loved her so much, why didn't I? I erroneously assumed the flaw was in me.

Healing Moment

 Toxic parents are too self-absorbed to sufficiently respond to the emotional needs of their children.

The loneliness of being and feeling unseen by our parents is as profound a pain as any physical injury; it just doesn't show itself on the outside. Gibson explains that emotional loneliness is a vague and private experience that is difficult for a person to conceptualize or describe. As children we have no way of identifying our parents as selfish, nor do we understand that our relationship with them is severely lacking closeness. Our young brains aren't mature or developed enough to form or understand the complexity and gravity of these types of concepts. As children we live in what we know. If we have feelings of loneliness, they are deep down inside of us. Gibson lets us know that this is how children experience their loneliness—as a deeply felt gut feeling. The loneliness we develop in our childhood most often continues into our lives as adults as evidenced by patterns of unconsciously choosing relationships that cannot offer us the emotional intimacy and levels of connection we're starving for.

To feel emotionally connected to and unconditionally loved and accepted by our family, especially our parents, is profoundly fulfilling. Gibson tells us it is this connected closeness that helps us develop a sense that we are loved for exactly who we are. This type of relationship can only be established when our parents seek to genuinely know us, not judge or manipulate us. When parents have the necessary self-awareness, they love nothing more than interacting with their children. It is the joy of their lives to experience life with their children and to genuinely know who they are as people. Healthy parents have an open-door policy when it comes to discussing and sharing emotions. If they have somehow hurt their children, their only desire is to do whatever it takes to talk it through and fix it. Attacking, being cruel, or cutting their children down would not enter the mind of a healthy parent. If, on some rare occasion, a healthy parent is unkind to their children, he or she takes the necessary steps to repair the shame they caused and own the responsibility for their wrongdoing.

Healing Moment

Healthy parents live their own exciting lives, are emotionally balanced, and are consistent in their attentiveness, love, and interest in their children. They are what their children need them to be—emotionally dependable.

Because our toxic parents didn't notice how we felt as children, or in my case they noticed but didn't care, the only choice we were given was to keep our feelings inside. This is a deeply isolating experience.

Gibson points out that to cope as children, we learn to do whatever is necessary to create some kind of connection with our parents. She states, "we learn to put other people's needs first as the price of admission to a relationship."[10] I can testify to this. When I was younger, I was a shameless pleaser in peer and romantic relationships. I desperately wanted to be loved so I pleased as a way to secure love and acceptance. This was a horrible habit I had to work hard to change as an adult and one I am still working on healing on some level.

As children, we learned far too young that we were not allowed to expect others to provide support or interest in us, so as a consequence we took on the role of being the giver and still take on this role. We don't think about healthy relationship concepts, such as mutuality or reciprocity. We over focus on if people think we're good enough and if people like us or not. If we get the idea that certain individuals we care for feel we're not measuring up, we go into overdrive to change whatever we believe they may not like about us to keep them from leaving. This is an empty and awful way to live. It often doesn't even occur to us that people are nice to us because they want *us* to like *them*. We have only had the experience of having to work hard to earn even the smallest morsels of love.

I have memories, both from childhood and adulthood, of my mother's reaction to me having needs or to me meeting my needs on my own. I saw a lot of eye-rolls and heard countless passive-aggressive digs that I wasn't giving her enough attention (especially if there was a man in my life). I witnessed her intensely begrudging attitude either in front of my face or performed behind my back for anything and everything she has ever given me. I have a memory of her coming out to California to help me move after my divorce. She contributed a significant amount of money to help my daughter and me get settled. She seemed genuinely happy to help, even held my hand while we shopped. She seemed genuinely excited to help us put everything together in our new place. Once we got home, I left to run an errand. My mother then looked at the friend of mine who had come over to help us set things up and said to him, "This is the last time I am ever going to spend this kind of time and money to help her out."

When I learned of the comment and confronted her about it, my mother gave me a swift dose of deflection. She accused my friend of being a negative person and a liar and that she couldn't imagine why he would ever say something like to me.

Here is what I have learned and what I teach daily in my office. Being genetically related to our toxic family members doesn't make us family. The real definition of family refers to constructs much deeper than bloodline or DNA. Family is about love, sacrifice, honesty, protection, support, unconditional love, reciprocity, acceptance, security, respect, protection, loyalty, and safety. It is not about cruelty, gang-up warfare, triangulation, manipulation, abandonment, lying, criticism, selfishness, betrayal, or gossip. When a family is full of these negative qualities, it is a family in name only. It is really merely a group of toxic people to whom we happen to be biologically related. No family is perfect, but not all families are plagued with deep patterns of superficial connections, destructive games, and psychological abuse. The psychological aspects of family should create a safe space for everyone to be wholly who they are. Family should create security, not break it down.

Healing Moment

 If our blood family is abusive, we have every right to open our heart and our life to new and healthier people capable of loving in the same ways we love. Doing this is not a betrayal. It's our right.

Lyric Therapy

No hope, just lies
And you're taught to cry into your pillow
But I survived
I'm still breathing
I'm alive
—"Alive," by Sia[11]

3

Toxic Mothers

There is a large misperception that females cannot be abusers. The fact is, many women, especially many mothers, are the source of intense relationship harm. Nevertheless, mothers manipulate a bit differently than fathers. Psychologically abusive mothers are sneakier, more covert and passive in their manipulations because they strive to hold up the billboard of a good mother to the public. This is not to say that no mothers are overtly abusive or violent. Certainly some are, especially if an addiction is involved. But most mothers thrive in the arena of emotional violence. Like all toxic people, a toxic mother's greatest flaw lies in her belief that everything revolves around her.

Keep in mind that when we are face-to-face with a toxic person, even the wisest, more secure adults usually experience feelings of confusion. Imagine, then, what it must be like for an innocent child who encounters the toxicity of her mother whom she loves and depends upon. Add to the fact that toxic mothers refuse to acknowledge their own failures by projecting their cruel thoughts and behaviors onto their children. With all of this at work, it is no wonder that children of toxic mothers misconstrue what is happening to them and learn to hate themselves. Self-hate is their only viable option because surely their mother cannot be bad.

Mother and the Development of Identity

I can say from personal experience and from treating many of my patients that there is almost nothing more confusing or painful than growing up under a toxic mother. Mothers have the most powerful influence on shaping our self-love and identity. Brenda Hunter's book *The Power of Mother Love* teaches us the depth of a mother's influence. A mother's love and emotional accessibility are essential to the development of feelings of well-being in her children. Her influence shapes our brain and contributes to us developing a conscience. She is our teacher of love. We learn directly from her if we are wanted or not, accepted or not, and lovable or not. Even if our mother has passed away, it is still her and our image of her that have a deep and lasting impact on how we view ourselves.

Brenda Hunter explains:

A child should never feel as if they need to earn a mother's love. This will leave a void in their heart all of their life. A mother's love needs to be given unconditionally to establish trust and a firm foundation of emotional intimacy in a child's life. If love is withheld, a child will look for it in a million other ways, sometimes throughout their lifetime unless they come to some sort of peace with their past. The emotional foundation we give our children at home is foundational to their life. We cannot underestimate the value of home and the power of a mother's love.[12]

When our mother is toxic, we quickly learn that the only way to attach to her is to be below her or strive to be the near perfect image of the child she is looking for. It becomes our task to take on all of her unfulfillable demands and neediness and to do exactly as she says. A toxic mother talks but never listens, and she gives advice but never takes any. And we have to deal with all of this because she's our *mother*.

Why Do They Have Children?

In an article written by Cindi Lopez,[13] we learn that toxic mothers do not have children for the same reasons healthy mothers do. Toxic mothers choose to have children for only one reason: to have more mirrors. Lopez contends these women have children so their children will love them unconditionally, not the other way around. They have children to use, manipulate, and control. They have children to have someone to do things for them. They have children who can go out and reflect the false image of what a good mother they are to the world. Toxic mothers may claim that motherhood is the greatest gift, but this is not true for them. They end up experiencing children as burdens. Lopez makes it clear that these women didn't expect that their cute, little, dependent babies would turn into unpleasant, ungrateful two-year-olds who have their own needs, minds, wants, and personalities. Toxic mothers want puppies who will love them no matter what, not real-life babies who grow up and can one day challenge them, expose them, and leave them. For healthy mothers, the most gratifying part of mothering is watching their children unfold in their own unique and independent ways. For a toxic mother, the natural passage of their children into their independence is experienced as an act of betrayal against her. If toxic mothers are not getting the attention they crave from their children, they experience their children as inconveniences who stand in their way of doing what they want to do for themselves.

Healing Moment

 Toxic mothers are image-oriented rather than love-oriented.

My mother's greatest irritation with me was I was the kid who expressed my sensitivities and discontentment with her treatment of me and with her consistent need to have a man in her life. My inability to thrive under all her selfish changes was an embarrassment for her. My reaction to her made her look bad; for this reason, she would insist I live with my dad because she allegedly couldn't handle me.

My telling her how I felt about her was considered "acting out." The more she would dismiss my feelings, the angrier I would get, the more I would act out, and the more she would pin the "crazy" button on me. She never saw my "acting out" as caused by her—not by her lifestyle or by her consistent need to be in control or by her going everywhere my brother was or by her lack of empathy toward me.

When I was eight years old, I was left with a babysitter while my mother went off with my brother to one of his athletic events. The sitter kept me out of making cookies with my stepbrother because I wasn't feeling well. She also left me alone while she went to the store to get ingredients for the cookies. While she was gone, I felt like I wasn't loved or important to anyone, including the sitter, so I grabbed my bubblegum-bear stuffed animal and left home. I walked in the snow to the grocery store that was a mile away from my house. There I sat on a rock where all the cars entered the parking lot. A woman in a station wagon pulled over and asked me where my parents were. I told her I wanted my dad. It was a small town, and she knew my dad. I got into her station wagon after telling her I wasn't supposed to go with a stranger. She told me I was safe with her and that she would take care of me. She held my hand and took me to my dad's office. Thank God I had angels watching over me.

My sensitive nature and my needs for my mother stood firmly in the way of her freedom. I didn't like her selfishness, and I let her know it that day. She hated me then and still hates me now for disliking her selfishness.

When we are raised by these types of mothers, we are always in doubt if we can trust if they were really toxic or if we were just too sensitive or too difficult to raise. Because of the fog this creates, I think it's important to describe the common traits found in these types of mothers to help define the problem and find clarity. When we see such descriptions, we start to feel validated in ways that ensure our perception of our relationship with our mother is founded in research, that we are not alone, that what we experienced is real, and that this same type of experience has actually been documented in the real world by people just like us. I remember when I read Morrigan's book *You're Not Crazy—It's Your Mother*, I felt like she had videotaped my life and then wrote her book about what she saw.

Never had I felt so validated and relieved, and also never more hurt and angry at the reality of who my mother really is. I hope the discussion that follows helps you as well.

Everything she does is deniable

Toxic mothers always have an excuse or an explanation for how they treat us. They are masters at couching their cruelties in loving terms. For example, their hostile and antagonistic acts are paraded as thoughtfulness, and their selfish manipulations are presented as gifts. Criticisms are slyly delivered as concern that they only want what is best for us, that all they want to do is help. Our toxic mothers are too wise to say to our face that they think we're inadequate. Instead, anytime we tell her we've done something great, she counters it with something our sibling did or what a friend's child did or something she did that was better. Or she may simply ignore us or hear us out without saying anything. Then, in a short time, she'll do something cruel to us so we understand not to feel too good about ourselves. In some cases, a toxic mother may actually acknowledge the excitement we feel by congratulating us. But beware: at the same time she shows her displeasure by congratulating us in a snide, annoyed voice, making her reaction totally deniable. It is nearly impossible to confront someone over their tone of voice, their demeanor, or the way that person looks at us. In a swift, passive-aggressive move, our toxic mother has delivered the message that we're not good enough.

Because our toxic mother's abusiveness is part of a lifelong campaign of control and because she is mindful to rationalize her abuse, we have an extremely difficult time explaining to other people what we find so awful about her. Make no mistake that toxic mothers are strategic about how and when they engage in their manipulative ways. The times and locations of their worst abuses are carefully chosen so that no one who might intervene will hear or see their bad behavior. My mother chose public places to provoke me into standing up for myself so she would have the opportunity to call me crazy in front of an audience. It would be impossible for a bystander who sees two people upset and raising their voices to know who was the provoker and who was acting in self-defense. I would leave these experiences feeling so awful about myself. My therapist has made it clear to me that when a plane is going down with me on it, I have every natural instinct and right to try to save myself. I have learned that, with my mother, I was having the natural reaction anyone would have to the abnormal situation I was placed in.

I love this quote: "Never argue with an idiot. People watching won't be able to tell the difference." When we are attacked and defending ourselves, we end up looking just as bad as our attacker, and our attacker will make sure to focus on only our reaction rather than what they did to cause our reaction.

Healing Moment

 Toxic mothers want us to think our normal reactions to their abuse are the problem, not the abuse itself.

Because toxic mothers are so skilled at covering up who they really are, their children almost universally report that no one believes them when they try to unveil the truth about their family situation. Unfortunately, therapists, given the deniable actions of the toxic mother and being unconsciously eager to defend a fellow parent, will often jump to the toxic mother's defense, reinforcing our sense of isolation and helplessness ("I'm sure she didn't mean it like that!"). I cannot tell you how many patients I have treated who have come from other therapists who only helped contribute to their problem. Toxic mother deniability is a frustrating and damaging behavior to experience and treat.

She violates your boundaries

Toxic mothers feel an entitlement to their children. Any attempts from their children at independence or personal freedom are strongly resisted. Some toxic mothers reluctantly allow normal rites of passage (learning to shave, wearing makeup, wanting to be with friends, getting a girlfriend), but if their children insist on such "privileges," their mothers punish them. I treated a seventeen-year-old girl who when she got her first job, her mother told her, "Since you're old enough to make your own money, I think you're old enough to pay for all of your own expenses."

If we communicate our needs for age-appropriate clothing, grooming, and control over our own life, our toxic mother accuses us of being disrespectful and proceeds to ridicule us for our needs. Independence to these mothers equates to being disrespectful. Because toxic mothers so overtly thwart our needs for autonomy, we end up feeling like extensions of them rather than independent persons with rights of our own.

Toxic mothers show their authority over us through their invasiveness into our lives in strange and subtle ways. One thing my food-obsessed mother did, without any thought for how rude it may feel, was constantly eat food off of my plate. Then she started doing this to my daughter. I remember my daughter asking me, "Why does Grammy always eat my food?" This was my mother's way to be invasive just for the thrill of it and to communicate that everything is hers. Other toxic mothers commit our time to things and people without consulting us, and will share who we are and what we think about life for us. One of the most humiliating things toxic mothers do is to discuss our "dysfunction" with others while in our presence while acting as if we're not there. This was a daily experience for me.

Toxic mothers can also be so deeply lacking in their awareness of boundaries that they will go as far as to keep tabs on our bodily functions and humiliate us by divulging this information to others. I had one patient whose mother was bizarrely focused on her menstrual cycle. Her mother would go through her trash to see how many tampons or pads my patient was using in a day. This mother complained to me how disgusting her daughter was because she didn't throw away her feminine hygiene in the trash *each day*, which, this mother claimed, made the bathroom smell. She also said that she couldn't bear sending her daughter to college when her daughter handled her menstrual cycle in such a dirty way because no one would want to be friends with her. This mother made such comments and performed such deeds under the umbrella of self-martyrdom and her "devotion" to caring about "how my daughter turns out." The reality was that she was ultimately resentful that her daughter was growing up.

Toxic mothers are known to ask nosey and invasive questions and to snoop through our mail, email, text messages, social media, letters, and diaries. They seek to "catch us" being up to no good so they can punish, degrade, and humiliate us for ruining the family name and our own lives. All of this is done without seeming embarrassment or thought. A mother of one of my young female patients was so invasive that she stalked her daughter on social media. She micromanaged every class her daughter took, consistently contacted her teachers, judged every friend she had, and turned her daughter's normal developmental phase through experimenting with alcohol or marijuana into her being an alcoholic and drug addict in need of rehab. She found every way she could to interfere with her daughter's life, including her going out with friends on the weekends, and she was overly critical of every guy this poor girl dated. If there was any normal conflict between my patient and a friend of hers, my patient's mother would immediately assume and accuse my patient of being in the wrong. All the while this mother claimed that she did all these things because of how deeply she cared for her daughter.

She undermines

Our toxic mother will only acknowledge our accomplishments as long as she can take some credit for them. My mother always used to boast, "Did you know athletic ability is inherited through the mother?" as her way to take credit for her superstar son. Any success or accomplishment for which she cannot take credit is ignored or diminished, which have been nearly all of mine. My mother can only take credit for helping to finance my life through my education and beyond to help get me on my feet. While I readily grant that she did this, the money was never freely given. She used it for manipulative control over me. It's common, of course, for parents who can to help their children throughout their lives, including financially. What isn't typical, much less healthy, is for parents to give money to their children in order to manipulate and control them for selfish ends.

Anytime our toxic mother knows we are going to be center stage for something while she isn't, she may try to prevent the occasion altogether, refuse to come, leave early, or act as if the event is no big deal. She may find ways to steal the spotlight, or she'll create opportunities to slip in little wounding comments about how much better someone else did or how what we did wasn't as much as we could have done. She undermines us by picking fights with us or through being especially unpleasant just before we have to make a major effort.

Toxic mothers act put out if they have to do anything to support our opportunities. My mother was the only mother who didn't support her daughter at our sorority initiation night. She neglected to write a letter about me for my sorority mom to read aloud during the event. I was hurt. I felt lonely and embarrassed as my friends and sorority mom tried to make me feel better. I was the only girl out of twenty-five who got nothing read to them that night, but my mother had no problem making it to every college sporting event of my brother's.

No matter what our successes are, toxic mothers have to take us down a notch. My therapist noted time and again that my mother hates it when I have nice things because she always finds a way to make my nice things bad. For instance, she noticed everything "wrong" with the home I purchased. She even shifted around my decorative pillows. On another occasion, she told me it had been all over the news that the airbags in my new car were faulty and were going to kill my daughter and me. I let her know a company as well known and successful as Mercedes would have sent me information or given me a phone call if there were issues with my car. My mother then told me I needed to go into the dealership because they weren't going to tell someone like me about car issues since I am "blonde and pretty." The subtext of her comments was that people think I'm stupid and are going to take advantage of me because of my appearance, but she, on the other hand, is just looking out for me. In reality, however, she was just cutting me down and trying to hurt me.

She demeans, criticizes, and belittles

Our toxic mother lets us know in all sorts of passive ways that she thinks less of us than she does our siblings and other peripheral people in our lives. If we complain about someone's mistreatment of us, she will take that person's side even if she doesn't know that individual. She doesn't care about those people or the fairness of our complaints. She just wants us to know that we're never right.

She will deliver generalized barbs that are almost impossible to refute and do this almost always in a loving, caring tone:

- "You were always difficult."
- "You can be very difficult to love."
- "When you were a teenager, I was ready to sell you for twenty-five cents or best offer."
- "No one could put up with the things you do."
- "Don't worry, honey, someone will marry you."

She delivers her barbs in an indirect way. For example, she'll complain about how "no one" loves her, does anything for her, or cares about her, or she'll complain that "everyone" is so selfish when we're the only person in the room. As always, she combines criticism with deniability. Toxic mothers are magicians at slipping little comments into conversations with us that they really enjoyed something they did with someone else—something she did with us too but didn't like as much. My mother did this to me all the time using my brother's wife as the person she preferred to be with because the two of them supposedly had "more in common." She would let me know that her relationship with my brother's wife was wonderful in a way my relationship with her wasn't—the carefully unspoken message being that I didn't matter much to her.

She makes you look crazy

When we try and confront our toxic mother on something she has done, she'll let us know that we're not remembering correctly. She accuses us of lying or of putting words in her mouth. Many toxic mothers will go as far as to tell us we must have very creative imaginations to come up with such fabricated stories about them.

Healing Moment

To have our experiences flat-out denied or otherwise invalidated is called gaslighting. Our perceptions of reality are continually undermined, causing us to lose confidence in our intuition, our memory, or our powers of reasoning.

Once our toxic mother has successfully constructed these lies about our emotional instability, she'll tell others about them, presenting her smears as expressions of concern and declaring her own helpless victimhood. Most recently, in an event that finally terminated a relationship with my mother, she told a close family friend and most important adult male influence in my life, "I don't know what gets into Sherrie. Out of nowhere she turns into some kind of a monster." My mother then told this man that she would be reaching out to my ex-husband, whom she overtly criticized from day one and hadn't reached out to in the many years since our divorce, to develop a relationship with him so she could see my daughter without my consent. She made good on her statement too. She does all of this because, in her world, she's innocent, she didn't do anything wrong, and she has no idea why I'm so "irrationally" angry with her. According to her, I have hurt her terribly, and she just loves me so much and would do anything to make me happy. But I'm so difficult that she's beside herself. She doesn't know what to do with me, so she has no other choice but to reach out to my ex-husband to triangulate my daughter. Clearly, a change in her own behavior is simply not an option.

In gaslighting like this, my toxic mother (at least in her own mind) instantaneously clears herself of any responsibility for my obvious hostility toward her, implying that there's something fundamentally wrong with me that makes me angry with her. In the process, she undermines my credibility with her listeners. She plays the role of the doting mother so perfectly that no one will believe me or anyone else who has a mother like her.

She's jealous

Toxic mothers live their lives festering in their incurable envy of others, including of their own children. Anytime we get something nice, our toxic mother becomes angry and envious, and her envy will be apparent when she admires whatever it is. She'll try to get it from us, spoil it for us, or get the same or better for herself. Even though she's our mother, she's in an unspoken competition with us. She's always working on ways to get what other people have and is verbally bitter of anyone whom she thinks has had it easier or better than she has.

She lies and fabricates

Toxic mothers lie in too many ways to count. In fact, it is questionable if they ever tell any realistic version of the truth. For a toxic mother, life is too boring without drama and histrionics added on top. When she talks about something that has emotional significance for her, it's fair to assume she's lying, withholding, or over exaggerating. These mothers are brilliant at taking a shard of the truth and bending it in every dramatic way possible to give it a whole new look that is more fitting to the emotional reactions they want to evoke.

If our toxic mother has recently engaged in something particularly egregious against us, she may engage in preventative lying: she lies in advance to discount what we might say before we even say it, just as my mother did in calling my ex-husband and reaching out to my most trusted family friend to label me a monster. My mother needed to jump in front of the truth and smear me to prevent anyone from believing my side of the same story, and to some degree what she did worked. She was believable enough to our family friend that I had to explain and defend myself to him for an hour. For me (not for him), this situation put a permanent fracture in our connection, which is exactly what my mother wanted to occur.

To those closest to our toxic mother, she'll blatantly lie. She will claim to be unable to remember bad things she has done, even if she did one of them recently and even if it was something very memorable. Of course, if we try to jog her memory by recounting the circumstances, we'll get a version of "That was so long ago" or "Why do you have to dredge up your old grudges?" or "It was just a fight, if you wanted to come back, you would be welcomed with open arms." Our conversations with her are full of casual brush-offs and diversionary lies, and she doesn't even respect us enough to bother making her lies sound good.

The most painful and frustrating lie to come from my mother is her telling people that I am narcissistic. For years I would question if I was this way because that is the last thing I would ever want to be. My therapist reassured me that if I even have the insight to ask that question that I am not narcissistic. My mother lies about my mental health to discredit me to her audience. The most painful piece of this is that people believe her.

The basis and goal of her lies is the same: to create conflict in the relationships between those she claims to love. She has not one issue with lying to people about what we have said, what we have done, or how we feel. She lies about her relationship with us, about our behavior, and about the reality of our situation with her in order to inflate herself and undermine our credibility while wrecking havoc in our relationships.

She has to be the center of attention

Neediness is a trait common to the large majority of toxic mothers. They view the very existence of their children as the sole source of getting attention and adoration. I treated a patient whose mother literally threw a tantrum in my office because her daughter didn't consistently ask her how she was doing at the end of each day, didn't thank her for every single thing she did, and didn't go out of her way to make her mother feel important. Her daughter was the absolute sweetest, most polite young woman, but she was never enough for her toxic mother.

Toxic mothers expect to be waited on. They load up their children with little requests: "While you're up …" Further, these mothers are the types who will assign a chore at the beginning of the week but will rage, throw tantrums, and heap up guilt on their children for not doing the chore on demand or at the most inconvenient time for them. Some mothers are more like the one I was raised with, who didn't assign any chores but made sure to make her doing the chores as guilt-provoking, dramatic, and martyring as possible to let me know just how much she does.

With toxic mothers, there is no such thing as enough. They will do just about anything to spoil any occasion where someone else is the center of attention, particularly the child they have cast as the scapegoat. My mother begged me to read one of her poems as a way to meet her need to be the center of attention at my doctoral graduation party. I refused to grant her this wish because we weren't even speaking the four days prior to the party due to a lie she told that involved my brother. While I was growing up, I watched her write poem after poem about my brother and his football career or about the house we grew up in. But never wrote one about me. She wanted to rub my face in the reality that I was not as important to her. At one point I asked her if she was ever going to write a poem about me, to which she said, "My mood has to be right to write one about you."

Our toxic mother will invite herself along when she wasn't invited. When she visits us or we visit her, we are required to spend all our time with her because entertaining herself is unthinkable. This is just another way she strives to remain the center of attention.

Toxic mothers are their own level of insanity.

She manipulates your emotions in order to feed on your pain

This trait is by far one of the worst. One of a toxic mother's favorite manipulative techniques is to feed off her cruelty. She will say and do things just to wound us while wearing a smile on her face. I have a memory of my mom making a comment about how the connection I share with my daughter is one she knows she has never had or shared with me. For a moment I thought she was actually complimenting me and noticing that she and I weren't close. Then she said, "Yeah, some kids are just a lot easier to raise like London has been." I was shattered. In one foul swoop she completely minimized my parenting and let me know she viewed me as a bad kid while I was growing up. No compliment anywhere.

These mothers commonly tease us about things we're sensitive about. For example, they may take us to scary movies and mock us for being scared. It's nearly impossible not to hear their smug laughter as they pressure us or say distressing things to us. Later they'll gloat over how much they upset us, happily telling other people that we're so much fun to tease and recruiting others to share in their amusement. As sad as this is, toxic mothers enjoy their cruelties and make no effort to hide them. They want us to know that our pain empowers them. They may bring up subjects that are painful for us and probe us about them, all the while watching us carefully for the hurt festering there. This is emotional vampirism at its finest.

She is self-absorbed

To a toxic mother, our needs and feelings come a very distant second to hers. She views her problems as deserving our immediate and full attention while ours are brushed aside. This is called role reversal. Her wishes always take precedence. If she does something for us, she reminds us constantly of her generosity and will often try to extract some sort of payment since a thank you is never enough.

My mother gave me free ski tickets one year. She paid nothing for them because she's given a handful of them every year from her old corporation. As I was about to leave for the day to ski with the man I was dating at that time, she continued to make comments about what a deal we were getting. She was so forceful and persistent that I asked if she wanted me to pay her for them. Later in the day she pulled the same antics after purchasing my daughter a ski lesson. I was so tired of hearing about it that I told her I'd pay her back. But she kept refusing to take any money from me while still acting as if I was the one putting her out. I was in yet another no-win situation with my mother.

Because toxic mothers are so selfish, one of their nearly universal characteristics is that they are incredibly bad gift-givers. They don't know us or anyone else well enough to give us what we want or need, and they don't want to give us anything as nice or nicer than anything they have. Most hurtfully, they will make it clear that it pains them to give us anything by consistently reminding us of all they have done for us.

She is overly sensitive
Toxic mothers have quick, defensive triggers. They are completely unable to take in any criticism about who they are or how they have behaved. When we try and confront our toxic mother on anything or if she feels we have defied her in any way, she will explode with fury, threaten, storm, rage, or even throw or destroy things. Some toxic mothers actually become physically violent, succumbing to beating us, confining us, putting us outdoors in bad weather, and engaging in other forms of physical abuse.

She threatens
Toxic mothers use fear as a powerful means to control their children. A toxic mother makes sure to make us feel fear even when we are not in her presence. We are so afraid of getting in trouble that it becomes easier for us to let her have her way. Even the adult children of a toxic mother still walk on eggshells around her. The fear of her tantrum just isn't worth challenging her in any way. Our toxic

mothers can turn their manipulation on with silence or a look that tells us they're thinking about how they're going to get even with us.

While not all toxic mothers abuse physically, many do and often in subtle and deniable ways. We may not have been beaten, but we were almost certainly left to endure physical pain when a normal mother would have made an effort to relieve our misery. This deniable form of abuse allows her to store up her rage and dole out punishment at a later time when she's worked out an airtight rationale for her abuse. For example, we may have been left hungry because "you eat too much junk." We may have been forced to go to school when sick just because we didn't "have a fever." I cannot even count the number of times my mother told me, "You're just trying to get out of school." The bottom line is that our toxic mother resents having to take care of us because it interferes with what she perceives she needs and wants to do for herself.

She is infantile and petty

Toxic mothers are immature and childish. If ever we refuse to let our toxic mother force us into doing something, she will cry that we don't love her because, if we did, we would do as she wanted. If we hurt her feelings, she will whine and make sure to tell us we'll be sorry when she dies and then realize we should have treated her better. These infantile complaints and responses may sound ridiculous, but our toxic mother is dead serious about them.

When we were children, if we asked her to stop being mean to us, she would justify it by pointing out something we did that she feels is comparable, as though the childish behavior of a child is justification for the childish behavior of an adult.

She uses revenge to settle the score. Revenge is a large part of her dealings with us. Anytime we fail to give her the admiration, attention, or service she feels she deserves or we spoil her wishes, she makes sure to show us her discontent.

Healing Moment

A toxic mother won't take no for an answer. She will do whatever is necessary to get us to give in, and we often yield to her just to keep the peace.

She "parentifies"

Toxic mothers shed their responsibilities as soon as they are able, leaving us to take care of ourselves as best we can. How is it that I had two parents formally educated to be schoolteachers, yet I almost failed fifth, eighth, and tenth grade? Because putting effort into helping me with my homework was nonexistent. They didn't think to check my grades until they were so bad that my teachers were concerned and my parents were forced to take action.

Some toxic mothers will deny us medical care, adequate clothing, or the necessary transportation. Others, like my mother, love having the attention of doctors and will take herself or her children to the doctor as often as possible.

Toxic mothers resent having to throw us birthday parties. They also hated if we had friends over, and they often made us the primary caregivers for young siblings. We may have had responsibility for excessive household tasks. Above all, we were given the job of being our toxic mother's emotional therapist, which is one reason any avoidance from taking on that role caused such enormous eruptions of rage from her.

We are never allowed to be needy or have bad feelings or problems. Toxic mothers reserve painful emotional experiences as solely for them, and we are held responsible for making those right. I experienced this throughout childhood. No matter the decisions my mother made, I was to go along and be quiet. She could have feelings about her divorces, but I couldn't. If I was mad, I only became a part of her problem. If a toxic mother is angry or upset, she expects the world to stop and for everyone to come to her rescue. The older we get, the more our toxic mother directly places responsibility for her welfare and her emotions on us, weeping on our shoulder and unloading on us anytime something goes awry for her.

She is exploitative

Many toxic mothers will manipulate other people to get work, money, or objects they envy, and they will expect to give nothing in return. This group to exploit includes their children, of course. My mother tried desperately to take a picture of a bird my daughter had painted because she wanted it for one of her bedrooms. No matter how many times my daughter and I denied her, she kept asking for it.

If our toxic mother setup a bank account for us, she made herself the trustee on the account with the right to withdraw money. As we put money into it, she took it out. I have a patient whose mother stole his identity and spent thirty thousand dollars on credit cards in his name. She even used that stolen money to take a pastor from her church to Europe. She told my patient that this pastor loved a statue he saw that was one thousand dollars while in Europe and she used the stolen credit card to buy it for him. She refused to pay my patient back, claiming he owed her that money for raising him and that she did something kind for a God-loving man, so how dare my patient complain.

She projects

Projection is a psychological defense whereby our toxic mother will displace her own bad behavior, poor character, and abusive treatment on us to deny them in herself. For instance, my mother tells people I am narcissistic. For years I wondered if she was right. But please hear this: if you even question whether you're the one who is narcissistic, understand that you are not. In fact, my therapist has helped me understand that I was not allowed to develop enough self-value growing up to even know I had a right, much less an ability, to say no when I needed to.

When we manage to refuse to be walked on, we provide our toxic mother with an opportunity to examine her behavior. But she won't take it. To her, that's an intolerable and unneeded situation. She doesn't think she has done anything wrong. So she transfers her "shame" onto our reaction, thereby justifying her truly abusive behavior. This bait-and-switch allows her to indulge in her childish willfulness by turning our forceful refusal to tolerate her poor treatment of us into a subject for further discussion: "We'll talk about this again later." Later will likely be when she's worn us down with her histrionics, pouting, and silent treatment thereby making us more inclined to do what she wants.

She is never wrong about anything

No matter what she's done, a toxic mother won't ever genuinely apologize for anything. Instead, when she feels pushed to apologize, she will sulk, issue an insulting apology, or negate the apology she has just made with justifications, qualifications, or self-pity:

- "I'm sorry you felt that I humiliated you."
- "I'm sorry if you feel I made you feel bad."
- "I'm sorry, but there's nothing I can do about it."
- "I'm sorry you feel embarrassed, stupid, and disgusting."
- "I'm sorry that my own child feels she has to be upset with me and make me feel bad."
- "I was just joking."

All of these varying so-called apologies are examples of projection. The words *I'm sorry* may be in her statement but the blame is still on us. Danu Morrigan accurately calls this a "fauxpology"—a fake *I'm sorry*.

Healing Moment

 What is missing in her apologies is the acknowledgment that what she did was wrong and what she will change about her behavior to make sure she doesn't hurt us like this again.

She has no empathy

It isn't that a toxic mother doesn't care at all about other people's feelings. It's that it would simply never occur to her to think about anyone else's feelings but her own. Even when someone is angry with her, she responds not with concern for the other person but with care only for herself. On the surface she may seem compassionate in her response. Inwardly, however, and soon outwardly, she will strive to justify herself, even at the expense of the person upset with her. Empathy requires genuine concern for another person. A toxic mother only cares about herself, making empathy impossible.

Healing Moment

An absence of empathy is the defining trait of having a personality disorder.

She blames

Toxic mothers are notorious for blaming us for all things that aren't right in their life. Such a mother will always, without fail, blame us for being the cause of how abusively she treats us. We upset her so much that she can't think straight. Things were hard for her and our backtalk pushed her over the edge. This blaming is often so subtle that all we know is that we thought we were wronged and now we feel confused, frustrated, and guilty.

My mother has made it a point to let me know how difficult I have been to love and raise, so if a boyfriend dumped me or I lost a friend, she can understand. After all, she has seen how difficult I am to love.

Our toxic mother will do something egregiously exploitative to us, and when we confront her, she will be annoyed with us, claiming that we're selfish to be upset at her for the "trivial" things she's done as she laments over the long list of all she has done for us that we still don't appreciate.

Healing Moment

Any negative reaction we give her, she will label as selfish, cruel, and unappreciative.

She destroys your relationships

Toxic mothers are like tornadoes: wherever they touch down, families are torn apart and wounds are inflicted. Unless the father has control over his toxic wife and holds the family together, the adult siblings characteristically have painful relationships. If communication is shared between siblings, it is usually superficial and driven by duty. Or it can be like communication between my brother and me—virtually nonexistent; we just don't talk to each other.

Toxic mothers nurture anger, contempt, and envy—the most eroding emotions—to drive their children apart from one another. While such a mother's children are still living at home, any child who stands up to her, which was me, gets pushed out. In her hunger for revenge, the toxic mother purposefully turns sibling anger on the "bad" sibling by including everyone in her retaliation. This is what my mother did through my brother's involvement in the gang-up warfare on my birthday for the writing of my story. She used my brother as her "protector" against me because I'm just so mean to tell the truth about our family.

The end result of being raised underneath a toxic mother is that almost all communication involves a third person. She is in the middle of the web, and she acutely and sensitively monitors all the children over whom she can maintain her self-centered role in the family. She then passes her patterns of abuse onto the others, creating the resentments that prevent them from communicating directly and freely with each other. The result is that the only communication between the children is through the toxic mother, exactly the way she wants it, even though she complains that she's so sad her children aren't closer.

While toxic mothers may never praise us to our face, they will likely brag behind our back about our victories to make them look good. Toxic mothers often won't compliment us to our face. My mother hardly ever asked about me directly. She almost exclusively only asked how my daughter was doing. If I wanted to be a part of our conversation, I would have to bring myself up, and she would quickly take what I was saying and somehow make it all about her and change the subject all together.

Toxic mothers tend to raise children who also suffer from envy. They raise children to feel like they aren't enough, which can make them envious that others have more than they do, even if that "more" is self-confidence or happiness.

She loves her illnesses

The majority of toxic mothers seem to have a large array of non-life-threatening illnesses or injuries. These all require medical attention and provide our toxic mother with all the attention she needs. She gets attention from the doctors she sees and requires us, as her family members, to run around and take care of her incessant, exaggerated demands. Her illnesses and injuries force us into her audience where we have to listen to her go on and on about what is wrong with her, how long it's going to take for her to heal, and all the care she needs in order to get better. She drives us crazy with her whining, talking, and complaining, which she distorts into claims that we never do enough and care enough and that we're abusive and neglectful toward her.

My mother drove the current man in her life so crazy over a surgery she had that he made my brother and I sign paperwork to take care of her if she ever got sick again. I have never known my mother not to visit some type of doctor less than twice per month. On one occasion she used an old walking cast to manipulate her way into getting a wheel chair at an airport to avoid standing in the TSA line, and then she boasted about it. It's insanity.

As a last resort, she goes pathetic

When a toxic mother is confronted with the unavoidable consequences of her manipulative behavior, which includes our anger, she will fall into a heap of soggy, weepy helplessness: "This is all my fault. I can't do anything right. I feel so bad." My mother literally said to me, "You have no idea how many days I spend in complete self-loathing." She said this to me on my birthday, the year after the birthday where I was annihilated for writing my book. I spent this entire phone call trying to make her feel better about herself.

What my mother doesn't do is own the responsibility for her horrible and spiteful behavior and make it right. Instead, as always, life is all about her. Her helpless, self-loathing, victimized tears dump the responsibility for the consequences of her poor treatment of us and for all her unhappiness about it onto us, her adult children. If we fail to excuse her bad behavior and make her feel better, we are the bad ones for being cold, heartless, and insensitive when our poor mother feels so awful.

When we try and explain this craziness to others, people say, "But she's your *mother!*" Why do people say this? Do they not realize that it only serves to make us feel crazier and more alone? Children of toxic mothers get discounted twice: first by their unloving mother, and then by the clueless people who invalidate the experience we have of her. These others invalidate us by saying, "Well, I am sure she had a good reason" or "You don't mean that ... of course you love your mother" or "Of course your mother loves you." Such people truly haven't a clue about the reality we live in.

Our society idealizes mothers. It is as if the moment we are born and we take our first breath, the woman involved in bringing us into the world is somehow sainted. For a healthier mother, this couldn't be truer. When I look at my daughter, I feel a combination of love and terror. She is my heart, but she's outside of my body walking vulnerably in the world. I only desire to love, protect, teach, and lead her. I've never had this experience with my mother, but it feels incredible to give it to my daughter. She is my Why in this life. She is why I work so hard, stay healthy, want to be the best, most stable, amazing woman I can be, set healthy boundaries, discipline myself, and let her experience independence. I see myself as her frame while she has all the room she needs to move around within its barriers. As my daughter grows, so does the size of her frame. Am I a perfect mother? No, I am not, but I am certainly good enough. I know this by how my daughter carries herself, by how happy she is, and by how many teachers and adults alike compliment me on how caring, smart, and loving she is. My daughter has good character, which is the most important thing I can teach her so she can elegantly, confidently, and gracefully navigate her life.

But this idealization of motherhood works against those of us who have toxic mothers. The assumptions that undergird it do not fit our mothers. They do not love us. They do not care about us or care for us. They seek no one's welfare but their own. And even what they think is good for them isn't. They are manipulative, destructive, blame-throwers, intolerant, infantile, and narcissistic. They care for no one but themselves. Biologically they may be mothers, but in no other way do they deserve that label. We wish other people realized this, and it would certainly help us if they did. But whether or not others understand the true reality of our situation, we must if we are ever going to find healing and happiness.

Healing Moment

Putting my daughter before myself is an honor, not an annoyance.

As devastating as it is to be in a relationship with a toxic mother, as an adult we do have options. We can explore our pain on the internet, with empathetic friends, and with professionals whom we hire to help us sort out the confusing quagmire of our feelings. Children, however, are young, vulnerable, dependent, inexperienced, and have no such options. Children believe what they are told, especially by their parents, so with toxic mothers children grow up believing that something is wrong with them when nothing could be further from the truth. The thing that is wrong with them is their toxic mother.

Lyric Therapy
I'm sorry mama
I never meant to hurt you
I never meant to make you cry
But tonight I'm cleaning out my closet
—"Cleaning Out My Closet," by Eminem[14]

4

Toxic Fathers

Toxic fathers tend to fall under the following categories: Tyrannical, Passive, and Overindulgent. These men are boys more than they are men. Toxic fathers, similar to toxic mothers, do not have any ability to be authentically available or present to their children because they're too consumed with meeting their own needs. If a toxic father is overly involved with his children, he typically has an agenda to live through them and dominate them. On the other hand, toxic fathers who are passive to our toxic mother walk on the same eggshells we do.

Characteristics of Toxic Fathers

Like toxic mothers, toxic fathers can be identified by what they say and do. Their behavior betrays the truth about their character. Mark Banschick, MD, an expert on divorce, provides a glimpse into the distorted, manipulative world of poisonous dads.

Self-centered

This is the father who is completely self-obsessed. He is vain and lives his life with an inflated sense of self-importance, which leads him to believe he's only entitled to the best of the best. This puts pressure on us as his children to be the best at whatever it is we excel at. To get close to our father, we often turn his interests into ours as a way to perform our way into his heart.

Uses people

Toxic fathers use people for their own good, especially their own children. A toxic father will use us to the point of exploiting us, if that suits him. He demands that everyone cater to him, and he treats people more like things rather than human beings with their own emotions, thoughts, and desires. If he sees no use for us, we will not get any of his attention.

When my father found out my brother was earning a substantial income, he asked my brother for a large sum of money to start a new business. My dad felt my brother owed him simply because he was his dad. My father never paid one penny of child support, so how did my brother owe him anything?

My dad entered into the health field later in his life and sold natural supplements, which is also a passion of mine. But if I wanted to take his supplements with any consistency, I had to pay him for them, although he never paid child support, provided no financial support toward any of my education, and entertained no thought to contributing anything to my wedding.

Like all toxic fathers, people, including their children, exist to be used for selfish ends, not loved, honored, or supported for their own sakes.

Charismatic

Toxic fathers have an all-encompassing energy about them—an energy that draws others to them like curious onlookers to a fire.

Our father was always at the center of attention, even when it seemed to us, his children, that he didn't seek it. It appeared as if people just fell at his feet and wanted to be part of his group. We often had fun watching our father bask in the spotlight, but each time we tried to engage with him while he was "on stage," he'd push us to the side. He just didn't have the time for us that we so wished he did. He put over his family anyone he could charm.

Grandiose

Toxic fathers have fantasies of success, prestige, and brilliance, but how they actually make money seems a complete mystery. Most of us who have been raised in toxic families only vaguely knew what our father did and could hardly describe his career to others. His magnificence was seductive and his achievements were often exaggerated while his ambitions often bordered on unrealistic. All we could see as children was that he was the boss and in control.

On the other side of this dynamic, yet lodged in the same toxic father, is the "poor me" man who may not make a lot of money but spends all of it on himself while claiming poverty to everyone who needs anything from him.

Rejects criticism

Nothing stings a toxic father more than criticism. People who go against him are either cut loose or verbally or physically assaulted. My father would walk out on my brother and me anytime we ever confronted him. We grew up watching him become verbally and physically violent with anyone who went against him.

Rage

The rage of a toxic father is truly scary. Some fathers are quick to anger and yell a lot. Toxic fathers can hurt their children with their anger in ways that cut to the bone.

I never knew from one minute to the next what mood my father would be in. He was a scary person. He yanked us around as kids if we weren't moving fast enough for him, and he had zero tolerance for us if things weren't done his way. He had no problem writing me horrible letters about what a bad person I was and how I was just like "the rest of my family." He had no problem cursing at me and calling me names. My father called me a "f*cking pr*ck" on my first day of college. I am thankful he was more out of my life while growing up more than he was ever in it.

Aloof and unsympathetic

Toxic fathers are unable to experience empathy. They completely disregard how we and others feel. Of course, our toxic father was completely in touch and sensitive to what *he* felt, but the feelings of his children were of no interest to him.

I treated a young patient who was by far the worst and most serious cutter I have ever worked with. In a family session, her father accused her of cutting herself because she wanted to be dramatic. His lack of care, his authoritarian approach to parenting, and the lack of empathy and support he offered my patient were the core causes of her behavior. When confronted with these realities, he refused to accept them. He saw no validity to the well-evidenced observation that he lacked empathy.

Absent

Toxic fathers get the majority of their gratification outside of the family. They tend to crave an excitement for entertaining others and are more concerned about what others think of them rather than having any concern for what their children think or feel about them. Toxic fathers view their children's love for them as automatic—something they deserve for just being fathers. They never consider that they might need to work for or nurture their children's love.

Other toxic fathers will hang out with their families more often than with friends. Because of their unlikable nature, they may not have many friends. But the more they are home, the worse it is for the family. When my father was home, everyone in the family dreaded it. He parented us with a "my way or the highway" mind-set and everyone had to follow suit. He got kicks out of bossing around everyone in the home. He savored having each of us under his control, doing exactly as he wanted.

There are also deadbeat dads like mine. My father was out living his own life while ignoring his children. We hardly saw him until he had the random desire to show up in our lives unexpectedly. And when he came, he expected us to feel graced by his presence. When I asked my dad if he was going to come to my high school graduation, he said he *might* show up. I looked for him the entire ceremony, but he never came.

Authoritarian

Toxic fathers don't consider the needs and interests of anyone but themselves.

In my home, if we spent time with our father, we had to spend our time doing what he wanted to do, doing things *he* enjoyed. He didn't care about taking part in our interests unless he could somehow narcissistically feed off of them, as he did with my brother's athletic life and career.

I treat two brothers who cannot stand seeing their father. Both boys forego spending any of their custodial time with him. For this, their father falsely blames their mother. This man would yell at the boys and degrade and embarrass them while they were actively playing in their sports. If my patients didn't follow his rules perfectly, perform perfectly, or respond to him perfectly, he created an all-out war against them. Both boys describe him as out of control, controlling, emotionally abusive, clingy, immature, and embarrassing.

Image-based

Toxic fathers care deeply about how others perceive them. They need us to look great to their friends, family members, and colleagues. We are only important to them if they can brag about us and take credit for being the father who raised such great kids.

Many toxic fathers play the role of the "cool dad" out in the world, but in the home they are neglectful and reactive, causing us to feel as if we're always walking on eggshells. I treat a male patient who is only nice to his children when in public but treats them as a complete annoyance in private.

I also treated a family where the father felt entitled to have an affair with the family's nineteen-year-old babysitter. Later he told his wife and children via public announcement that he wanted to divorce his wife on the day of their twenty-fourth wedding anniversary. He chose this day because he didn't want to have sex with her on their actual anniversary, although it was okay for him to have sex with her two days prior. He also held the incredulous belief that he and his wife could be best friends and raise their two girls together going forward. This father ended up losing everything, including the large majority of his friends. To this day he seems completely bewildered as to why and continues to place blame on everyone else. He erroneously believes his reputation has been tarnished by others and by their lack of understanding rather than that his reputation was destroyed as a result of his own actions. He is totally aghast over why his friends think he's wrong and why his children cut him off. In one of our sessions, he said to me, "C'mon Sherrie, every man does the babysitter." He saw it as my job to cleanup his mess and save his reputation.

He also sent me many emails dictating how I should be doing my job. Since I am not paid to be emotionally abused by my patients, I terminated him. Consequently, my name found its way into this man's divorce paperwork. There he has it specified that he will never pay for my treatment of his girls. The court-ordered therapist he requested only affirmed my views around the destructive nature marital affairs have on the relationship between parents and the perception their children have of them after they are discovered. Affairs parents have on their spouse often permanently destroy the relationship the cheating parent has with their children. This man quit going to the court-ordered therapist soon after getting that feedback.

Since the divorce, he remarried very quickly, and the new woman in his life reached out to me on Facebook accusing me of being unfair to her husband, poisoning his girls against him, and encouraging his ex-wife to do the same. Insanity.

This toxic father and husband was not sorry for what he had done to his family and to me, and much of the correspondence I witnessed between him and his girls was geared toward convincing, lecturing, and preaching to them that he was in the right and his role as their father should supersede any of the hurt and disruption he caused them. He was more focused on his "rights" as their father than on having any interest in genuinely tending to their hurt, shock, betrayal, and disbelief. Parents should never treat their children as property to own rather than as human beings to love, cherish, and care for. This man needs to be reminded that it takes years to build a reputation and only one bad mistake to lose it forever. His children may love him again one day, but they will likely never again have any respect for him.

Selfish

Because a toxic father is inherently egocentric, his children cannot get what they really need from him so they can develop into whole, confident individuals. He's too self-involved to give his children anything but the leftover scraps of his time and attention.

Money tends to be a toxic father's god. Toxic people who cannot love people, start loving money. They love money as a way to possess things and establish control. The more money they have, the more things they can possess and the more people they can control. The problem is that money is not a path that leads to deep contentment and connection. These fathers may have control and power, but they do not and cannot give love. Deep contentment only comes from loving a person. Money will not reject a toxic father, but it also cannot respond to him and that is the problem.

These men falsely assume that when they use their money to give their children nice things, they have emotionally satisfied them. The reality, however, is that the material gifts of toxic fathers can never substitute for the love they refuse to give their children. A child craves and needs love, especially the love of her father and mother. When a toxic father gives things rather than love, his children end up granting little value to his substitute treats. When his kids are not perfect and happy in response to his gifts, he becomes angry and accuses them of being ungrateful, entitled, spoiled kids who do not appreciate or respect him. If he doesn't get the compliance or reaction he is looking for, toxic fathers commonly threaten to take away the gifts as a follow-up means of establishing control.

Further, everything a toxic father gives he later uses to produce feelings of guilt, obligation, or obedience in those he "loves." He may provide on the material level, but his children are mostly left feeling deprived on an inward level. The only way to secure a toxic father's attention is to be around on the rare moments he feels like giving it.

I worked with a young man whose high school did a drunk driving exercise where certain kids were chosen to fictitiously die. This program's intention was to teach kids the importance of not drinking and driving. My patient had to write a goodbye letter to his parents, and he had to read his obituary at his fictitious funeral. The parents were supposed to write something back to their son on the goodbye letter he had written to them, and they were to attend the funeral service for him the next day at the school. My patient and all the other students took this exercise very seriously. It was emotional for all of them. But my patient's father thought the exercise was stupid and refused to participate. My patient was devastated. His father's disinterest and insensitivity created a wedge between father and son that will likely never heal. A few months later, this father bought my patient a new truck. The new truck didn't make up for his lack of emotional involvement in my patient's life, but it sure made the dad look good.

Toxic fathers give in order to get. They need to feel superior. They need to feel as if everyone is inferior to them and that they have the power, with their money, to control and dictate to everyone around them. This is called financial abuse. Toxic fathers are self-centered and seek the aggrandizement of others. Those under their "care" are mere means to their selfish ends.

Types of Toxic Fathers

Similar to toxic mothers, toxic fathers view their children as extensions of themselves. They do not see or validate their children as unique or separate individuals with their own thoughts, minds, or needs. They are fathers who live from a weak sense of self and use their poisonous behaviors to overcompensate for their deep insecurities. They view their children as perfect, dependent, and vulnerable people to manipulate. And like toxic mothers, toxic fathers come in various shapes and sizes.

Tyrannical Fathers

When we are raised under a father who is overtly or covertly bullying us, it is incredibly hard to feel a sense of safety. Whereas mothers are nearly sainted once they give birth, many fathers are experienced as scary and threatening. With a tyrannical father, their children know that any *real punishment* they will incur will come down from up high once father comes home. And even when punishment isn't expected, a toxic father's mood is so unpredictable that family members scatter when he walks through the door.

A tyrannical father is more interested in whether his children obey certain rules than in having any interest in what his children feel, think, or have going on in their lives. Such a father also has high expectations when it comes to how his children perform, but he has virtually no empathy for how his children feel. He doesn't really care if they are struggling or not. He views their emotions as petty and dramatic and not worth acknowledging as genuine or significant.

Tyrannical fathers impact sons and daughters differently. Let's consider their daughters first.

Their Daughters

Author and expert in narcissism Alexander Burgemeester writes that daughters of toxic fathers report deep feelings of loneliness and abandonment when asked about their fathers.[15] Because our toxic father was so self-consumed, we never got enough time with him to feel like his pretty princess. If anything, we felt like we had to compete for his attention with our siblings or with others. When we were younger, our toxic father may have told us how pretty we were, but as we got older, he rarely missed an opportunity to comment on our weight and "poor" attitude.

I will never forget the day at a track meet when my father appeared out of nowhere. I hadn't seen him in two years. He showed up with some new woman in his life who looked starved to death. One of the first things he said as I was about to go out and compete was that I had gotten "fat" because I was eating too much bread. I never asked his opinion about my weight, and given his two-year absence, he was truly ignorant of my diet so had no informed basis for making that comment. Not only was my father hard on me about my weight, but he was hard on all women. If an overweight woman walked by, my father would make horribly disgusting and derogatory comments about her. I am certain that his fat phobia was one of the many contributors to the development of the eating disorder I had as a teenager and the lingering poor body image I had for years after my recovery.

In a clinical case of mine, I was treating two sisters whose father made their lives a living hell. He never validated them as beautiful, useful, smart, or worthy of love or being valued. He treated them like secondhand slaves. If they wanted anything from him that would cost him money, they were told to write business proposals for those things. He stole their identities from them by taking anything he gave them, including the rooms they slept in. He told them, "That's not yours; I paid for it." This was just one of his favorite ways of exacting revenge on his daughters when they behaved in a way he found disagreeable. Both of these girls have body image, self-worth, self-doubt, and relationship challenges as consequences of living under their tyrannical father.

Even daughters who are otherwise successful often carry ravaging, poisonous consequences into adulthood. The destruction sown in their childhood follows them as they move away from home, date, marry, raise children, pursue a career, and strive to do anything else in their lives. Their father drove into their hearts the stake that nothing they do can ever be good enough. Their future relationships with men are largely plagued with feelings of vulnerability and insecurity because they do not believe they are lovable at their core. Some of these daughters anxiously avoid commitment. Some take on the toxic role in relationships as learned ways to maintain relational distance or cause relationships to never form beyond the superficial. They often take such measures for self-protection, but these choices certainly don't lead to healthy relationships.

Their Sons

Burgemeester writes that sons of toxic fathers feel they can never measure up. Their fathers were so competitive that they would even compete with their sons. Toxic fathers fluctuate between extremes with their sons. They compete against them or pay them no attention at all. Some sons can feel so deflated that they stop competing at all because they come to believe that their father is too big and much more skilled than they are to possibly beat him. Other sons work hard to beat them their father. And when they finally win, they receive for their efforts a father who rages at them and humiliates them for their success. He accuses them of cheating or claims, "Don't get a big head; I let you win."

Because sons of toxic fathers never feel good enough, they feel empty or second rate deep in their heart, even when they do succeed. These boys grow up feeling valued or loved only for how well they perform or follow commands rather than for who they are as persons. My father was certainly this way, and it had a negative impact on my brother. I have no doubt that my brother wonders why anyone loves him. And when expressions of love come his way, he wonders if it's because of who he is as a person or only because he was a world-class athlete and successful businessman. Sons of fathers like this grow up never knowing the why behind people loving them. This makes sons of toxic fathers insecure and in need of a lot of reassurance in their relationships, which can in essence make them toxic since all the love and adoration from those they choose to love must be due to their doing, not to their being. These sons feel they are loved because of their performance, not because of who they are. So the destructive cycle continues.

Toxic fathers, like toxic mothers, are deeply damaging to their children. They disregard boundaries, manipulate their children by withholding affection (until the children "perform"), and fail to meet the needs of their children because they are only concerned with their needs being met first. There is a profound unhappiness among the members of a family ruled by a tyrannical and bullish father. In many of these families, the mother simply acquiesces to the father's demands because she has been beaten down so far inside of herself that she lives feeling confused and uncertain about everything. She has lost touch with her sense of self and the validity of her own ideas and opinions. Often this destructive pattern had its start in the mother's own childhood. This leaves her helpless to protect herself or her children, and she lives in the guilt of not having the confidence to leave and do better for herself and her children.

Healing Moment

 In the family system, if it is sick at the top, the trickle-down effect is that it will also be sick at the bottom.

Passive Fathers

Tyrannical fathers are scary and unpredictable to their children.

Passive fathers don't produce such a hard, direct hit on their children's egos or emotions as tyrannical fathers do. Passive fathers tend to engender a serious lack of respect and a great deal of frustration in both sons and daughters.

The passive father is perhaps the most pathetic of all toxic fathers. He is the man who doesn't have a backbone against our toxic mother. In her book *You're Not Crazy—It's Your Mother*, Morrigan makes it clear that passive or enabling fathers will not protect us, and rarely, if ever, will they rock the boat to defend us. The passive father's thought of going against his wife brings up such deep fear or dread that he stays silent, or out of his fear, he may even actively assist in our abuse and disparagement. Other passive fathers choose to ride both sides of the fence by fence-whispering to us in private that he understands our pain while urging us to do as our toxic mother wishes, putting up with her abuse, so our life will get easier. To make his own life peaceful, a passive father often turns to us, his children, to make peace with our toxic mother even after he bears witness to her blatant and unfair treatment of us. He tells us to "forgive and move on." As his children, we need him and our toxic mother so we are blinded to the lack of logic in his requests.

I work with a young female patient who has a father locked into a marriage with her alcoholic, pill-popping, emotionally violent mother. My patient cries daily wishing her father would just leave her mother and find some level of happiness in his life. Her father looks aged beyond his years due to the stress of being with her mother and all the chaos she creates for him. Her mother is emotionally erratic and physically, verbally, and financially abusive of him. Her parents also share a dependent special needs child who adds to her father's pressure. On top of all this, he sees a divorce with her as financial suicide, knowing his wife will be as vengeful as possible if he were to ever leave her. Her father, for the most part, puts his arm around his wife and acts like the craziness she is exhibiting isn't happening, even when it's going on right in front of him. To her complete devastation, my patient is coming to understand it is easier, not happier, for her father to stay with her toxic mother. This leaves my patient in the position to be able to only have a remnant of a connected relationship with her father in private because her mother rages at the closeness she and her father share. So her relationship with her father is based in secrecy and lies.

Sadly, the passive father lives a life that is not his own. He tends to be conflict-aversive and to use external doctrines, such as from religious teachings, for his reasons to stay married to his toxic wife. He refuses to cross her in any way, which includes suggestions for her to get therapy, enter rehab, be subject to an intervention, or use any other source that could possibly help the marriage. The toxic wife sees nothing wrong with her and stands in direct refusal to get any help.

Overindulgent Fathers

The father who overindulges his children, whether married or divorced, raises self-centered children. This is the father who either lives vicariously through one or more of his children, or he's so distant and uninvolved with his children that the only way he can comfortably connect with them is to have no rules and to please them by giving them everything they want. Whatever the case may be, the pattern he sets up is one in which the tail wags the dog. The children say "Jump!" and daddy asks "How high?" In this dynamic, the word *no* is not in the overindulgent father's vocabulary. His children may love him, but they have no respect for him. In effect, he raises children to become demanding, spoiled, and obnoxious.

I treated a son whose father overcompensated for him so much as he was being raised that he was required to do very little work in his life to find himself and a sense of his own independence. He was grandfathered into a very successful family business where he was not required to pursue any sort of an education. He began working under his parents from a very young age alongside his two other brothers. By the time he married and had kids of his own, he had developed an addiction to alcohol and pills, was resentful of his more successful, more adored younger brother, and lost all motivation to perform at work. His father saw him as the big disappointment. After some time in treatment with me, he realized he had been overindulged and not ever encouraged to pursue anything other than a career in the family business. It didn't matter to this patient of mine that he made good money. He wasn't happy. His addictions took over his life so powerfully that there needed to be an intervention.

He is now sober and still working in the family business, but he is traveling more, working on his sobriety and health, connecting with God, family, and his children, and learning to take a more individual and responsible hold over his life. Many people in his situation fail to do this and live their lives lazy, miserable, unmotivated, entitled, and addicted.

The Missing Pieces

Whoever our toxic father was, whether he was tyrannical, passive, overindulging, or absent, we grew up with a missing piece of our self-identity. We missed out on the love, care, and leadership that a healthy, stable father offers his children. This is devastating for both boys and girls who crave the fantasy of the father they never had. No father is perfect, but there are plenty of fathers who deeply love their children and who give them the necessary and appropriate support and discipline, equipping them to venture out into their lives feeling good enough about who they are so they can become independent and successful.

Healthy parents understand that disciplinary action is what holds the most influence over their children. They use it sparingly, wisely, and lovingly to provide correction for the sake of their children. As a result, their children grow up knowing they are loved, who they are, why they are, and how to flourish in life. Their adult children make mistakes, struggle, and suffer hurts, but they always know that home is a safe, secure, and nourishing place to return to and find good counsel when needed. The more reactive emotions—such as anger, tears, or shutting down—have almost no negative influence over the behavior of children raised in a healthy, supportive, loving environment.

None of this is true in a home with toxic parents reigning at the center of it. When children perceive that their parents cannot control their own emotions under stressful circumstances with them, they never develop the necessary respect for their parents that is essential for them to learn, mature, and grow into healthy people. Parents represent the justice system to their children. When parents are on the verge of raging, of breaking down into tears, or heading into a complete emotional shut-down instead of taking appropriate and healthy disciplinary actions with their children, their children lose respect for them. Children perceive parental frustration as a flaw that exists within their parents. Children come to view their parents as incapable of managing and controlling their own lives. Think about it like this: Would you respect a court judge who behaved in any of the ways toxic parents do under stressful circumstances? Certainly not. The judicial system is designed to be objective, rational, dignified, and fair-minded, and it is focused on protecting victims while bringing punishment to bear on those who victimize. Shouldn't children receive at least this much from their parents?

Toxic fathers are unjust, selfish, irrational, undignified, undisciplined, unfair, immature, and harshly bear down on those they should be loving and supporting. They crush their children in countless ways. But we can rise from the harm they have done. We do not have to remain under their domination. And this healing path starts with recognizing and accepting the truth about our fathers and what they did to us. We did not deserve the damage they caused, and we don't have to let it go on hurting us.

Lyric Therapy

Paranoia, what did I do wrong this time?
That's parents for you
Very loyal? Shoulda had my back
But you put a knife in it—my hands are full
What else should I carry for you?
—"Let You Down," by NF[16]

5

Toxic Adult Children

S uccess.
Happiness.
Fulfillment.

These are the hopes and dreams that most parents have for their children as they see them enter the world.

However, there are times when these hopes and dreams do not manifest because parents fail to provide their children with the important things they need to develop into disciplined, patient, kind, thoughtful, and hardworking people. Not all these children are the consequence of toxic parenting. Some, however, are. And the issues they deal with profoundly affect them for the rest of their lives.

Toxic children, for one reason or another, do not mature. In her book *Healing from Hidden Abuse*, Shannon Thomas explains that overindulged children feel as if normal societal rules do not apply to them but only to other lowly, "regular" people. Overindulging parents who have raised toxic children tend to have bent over backward to deny or cover-up for any and all of the mistakes their children made. As a result, toxic adult children come to view other people, especially their parents, only as objects whose sole purpose in life is to make things easier and less stressful for them. Overindulging parents forgot to remind their children that they stand among the billions of other ordinary people in the world. They have taught their children to view themselves as more special and unique than others, and because of this, these toxic children feel permitted to have whatever they want when they want it regardless of how other people may feel about it. Toxic children do not believe *they* need to change—they think the *world* needs to change. This flawed belief system sets them up to enter into adulthood entitled, demanding, critical, and emotionally immature. They expect life to be easier than it is. Whether these kids are successful or not doesn't really matter. What matters is the pattern of entitlement, selfishness, and self-adoration they live in.

On the other side of that experience, Thomas explains that other toxic adult children grew up in homes that were not overindulging. They may have been raised in cold and mechanical environments where parents did not meet their needs for genuine and loving attachments. These children decided that, once they were old enough to meet their own needs, they would turn it into a game of "having theirs" at all cost. These toxic adult children view life and people as owing them. Their insatiable appetite for getting what they view as rightfully theirs only causes them to want more and more of whatever other people have to offer.

Whichever side these toxic children were raised on, whether they got too much or too little, they treat other people with zero respect. They expect others to fall in line with taking care of their every whim and need. If we don't acquiesce to their demands, we will be met with unreasonable behavior, revenge, abuse, and abandonment. Toxic children have learned to use people rather than to love or appreciate them. They are self-centered, in love with their own image, their needs, and wants, and, like other toxic people, don't care about anyone but themselves.

The emotional immaturity of toxic adult children becomes harder and harder for others to tolerate as these children age. Their immaturity and demanding ways become more repulsive to people who are expecting to deal with a person who has appropriate levels of maturity and thoughtfulness. As adults, toxic children have a hard time keeping friendships or relationships of any kind. They also find it a struggle to get ahead in their careers. Their spoiled attitudes eventually destroy everything they try to make their own. They are forced to consistently start over with a whole new set of friends, lovers, and jobs, and they repeat this cycle throughout their lives.

If, as parents, we consistently clean up the messes our children make, continue doing everything for them to avoid conflict or to selfishly avoid our own feelings of guilt, our children only become more toxic. All human beings need what is called "optimal levels of frustration" to develop into healthy, caring adults. For children to grow into wise, mature, highly functional adults, we must provide them with an ideal, non-traumatic frustration of their needs that will foster new learning and personal development. We must exercise appropriate control and communication with them when it comes to expecting reasonable levels of achievement from them and to let them know when their needs for independence may be leading them down the wrong path. We must teach our children that life can be difficult and that even the most loved and nurtured children are going to get physically and emotionally tossed around by life from time to time. Experience coupled with adversity provides our children the opportunity to learn the various ways to cope when challenges arise. As parents, we should strive to keep their frustrations to a minimum and explain and soothe our children as best as possible when frustrations cannot be avoided. This is how frustration is optimized. We must be mindful not to rob our children of the very frustrations they need to help them grow.

At some point, it becomes too late to discipline toxic children. Depending upon how destructive they act out, this unfortunately places some parents in the sad task of having to cut ties with them. When this happens, usually the best teacher for toxic adult children is life itself. Some toxic adult children will learn and grow from their life experiences and even feel remorse for how they have treated other people. Others, though, will miss each life-lesson offered to them and continue to spiral down into their own destructive self-centeredness.

Eight Guaranteed Ways to Mess up Your Children

In 2014, I wrote an article for the *Huffington Post* on the eight guaranteed ways to emotionally mess up our children. It received a lot of attention and generated a good deal of discussion because our society seems to be struggling with this new entitlement-minded generation of toxic children. If these eight parenting techniques are the norm in the family system, toxic children will be the result.

1) Ignore or minimize your child's feelings

If a child is expressing sadness, anger, or fear, and parents mock, humiliate, ignore, or tease him, they minimize the importance of what the child is trying to tell them. Parents essentially give their children the message that what they feel is wrong and insignificant. When parents do this, they withhold love from their children and miss opportunities to develop open, vulnerable connections with them, which are necessary for children to experience so they learn how to bond and to love and be loved unconditionally. If parents don't care about how their children feel, they run the great risk of raising children who learn not to care about how other people feel.

2) Inconsistent rules

If parents never discuss expectations with their children, they keep their children from learning how to behave appropriately. Children live up or down to what parents expect. Rules give children guidelines and boundaries that help them define who they are, both good and bad. If parents keep their children guessing and then punish them for letting them down, life becomes vague and unpredictable for them. Children will work to find their boundaries and discover the rules. Some of them will do this through acting out, then looking to see how their parents react in order to discover what they have not made clear.

Parents who fail to communicate rules to their children create an environment of ambiguity that leaves kids scrambling to bring clarity to it. But the ambiguity gives parents who act more irrationally and inconsistently the freedom to be who they are without regard to what their children need from them. This approach to parenting sets up children to suffer from low self-esteem and problematic behavior.

3) Make your child your friend

It is important for parents to refrain from sharing all their worries, concerns, and relationship problems with their children. Parents also must not consistently ask their children for advice on adult issues. If parents act helpless and defeated to their children, their children will never learn to respect them. Instead, children will start treating their parents as equals or even as inferiors because they feel the burden to parent their parents' emotional needs. Being friends with our children may be more appropriate as they age into adulthood. However, with my daughter I see myself as playing two roles. One role is "mom." When I am in the mom role, it is the more relaxed, playful, and joking part of our relationship where we can be friendly, lighthearted, and goofy. This role has many of the loving elements of friendship. The other role I play is "mother." In the mother role, I am her leader, healer, mentor, disciplinarian, listener, nurturer, and solution-finder. The mother role is always present, even when I am in the mom role. My daughter, no matter how playful and goofy we are together, knows I am the governor of our dynamic with respect to me and the expectations I have of her as central to our relationship. I never want my daughter to view me as her equal since it gives her nowhere to turn when she's in need of her mother.

Our child is not our friend. And we are not our child's friend. This does not mean friendliness is not an integral and important part of our relationship with them. Nevertheless, our role is different, more profound, more challenging, and carries with it much more responsibility. We must look after our children, teach them, support them, discipline them, care for them, and help them figure out who they are, why they are, and what they can achieve in life. We must also model for them what it looks like to face life's challenges and how to navigate through times of stress and uncertainty and come out on the other side more confident and knowledgeable persons.

It's okay to be real with our children and to experience our emotions, but it is not okay to burden our children with them.

4) Put down your child's other parent

If a parent never shows affection and love to their partner in front of their children, their children will not develop a barometer for what love is or what love should look like. If parents are always putting their spouse down and rejecting him or her or threatening divorce, they create a chronic state of anxiety in their children.

Furthermore, if parents have already divorced and remain cold, distant, bitter, and angry, and one or the other or both blame each other for what happened, they send a message to their children that the ex-spouse is the cause of the divorce and the other parent should be their children's preferred parent. This can lead to parent alienation, where a parent poisons their children to dislike and not want to see their other parent.

As parents we cannot control if our ex-spouse is, in fact, deficient or blameworthy. What we must give our children is the space to come to that knowledge on their own, and then they can make their own decisions about us and our partner and how they are going to respond.

5) Punish independence and separation

When parents punish their children for growing up, they make their children feel guilty for having normal developmental needs and desires. This causes in them deep insecurity, rebellion, cutting, and other forms of behavior that indicate a failure to branch out and be themselves as independent people.

I treated a young female patient whose mother felt abandoned and bitter because my patient was growing up. This mother over-controlled her daughter's life to a point that the daughter felt like she was suffocating. The mother approved of nothing in her daughter's life that brought her into a sense of her own independence, whether that was her friends, her clothing, her boyfriends, having a car, or even getting a job where she could make her own money. This girl lived with chronic feelings of guilt and confusion and engaged in rebellious behavior and lying as ways to experience a sense of independence. The mother, on the other hand, was more savvy than an FBI agent. She caught her daughter in each and every trespass and punished her mercilessly through guilt and humiliation. On many occasions the daughter reported feeling hopeless and suicidal. I watched this mother-daughter dynamic repeat itself over and over. The mother was unable to take any feedback in therapy and consistently sought to prove there was something organic going on in her daughter's brain chemistry.

The mother didn't seem to grasp the fact that the need her daughter felt for independence was not a mental illness.

6) Treat your child as an extension of you

If parents link their own self-image and self-worth to their children's appearance, performance, behavior, grades, how many friends they have, how popular they are, and if they have all the trendy clothes and gadgets, these parents covertly give the message to their children that they are not loved for who they are but for how they look or how well they perform or what they own. Parents need to keep in mind that their children do not owe it to their parents to build or maintain the image of them that they want publically. Parents need to be able to stand alone and confident in their own identities.

7) Meddle in your child's relationships

When parents direct every detail of every choice their children make in their relationships—from friends to teachers—it inhibits the development of their maturity. For example, if our children get in trouble at school and we immediately rush to talk to the teacher to get them off the hook, or we constantly tell our children how to be a friend and who to be friends with, they will never learn to navigate on their own the sharper edges relationships bring.

8) Overprotect

When parents protect their children from every problem and emotion, they create a sense of entitlement and inflated self-esteem in their children that often crosses the line into narcissism. Parents teach their children to expect life to be more effortless than it is and raise them to want everything done for them regardless how they behave or if they have earned it. This type of parenting sets up children to feel depressed, defeated, and confused when they don't get the things in life they feel they deserve. Their superiority complex becomes so distorted that they believe the world revolves around them. When they experience times in life when things are boring, their minds shut down and they move onto something else that holds more promise of garnering them the praise and attention they crave.

These children are raised to be sore losers, and they will immediately abandon projects that won't make them shine.

Healing Moment

When parents treat their children with affection, discipline, and appreciation, their children internalize the truth that they are special and valuable but not superior.

"Daddy's Girl"

Another great example of an entitled toxic adult child is the all too common enmeshed "daddy's girl." I wrote an article about this phenomenon for the *Huffington Post* in 2015. I briefly dated a man who shares this dynamic with his daughter, and it was shocking to me to witness it and sad for them both. This is also a dynamic I have seen between some mothers and their sons. This pattern can also flow from a male parent to a male child or from a female parent to a female child. Either way the direction leans, the results in the children are the same. So while I'll center my focus here on dads and their daughters, realize that the pattern is not gender dependent.

There is a lot of romance around being a daddy's girl. The common notion is that daddy's girls are adored, spoiled, and mentally and emotionally healthier than girls with less involved fathers and choose healthier men to love as they mature. However, the reality is that, in an unhealthy daddy's girl situation, the relationship between the father and his daughter has every quality of a romantic relationship, minus the deeper levels of physical intimacy. Their relationship is based in equality where the father doesn't hold the position of the respected authority. In fact, it's quite the opposite. This kind of father/daughter relationship is mutually parasitic and destructive. This is parent/child enmeshment. The individuals involved would be better off and healthier without the other one in the picture.

In contrast, a healthy father/daughter relationship involves fathers raising their daughters to be classy, well behaved, modest, and kind to others. The father raises his daughter to become her own person—to make her own decisions and live her life with or without him. Love abides between them, but a love that is other-centered, not self-centered.

Let's look more closely at the toxic side of an unhealthy daddy's girl relationship.

The enmeshed daddy's girl

When the relationship between father and daughter becomes a toxic entanglement, the father makes a "star" of his daughter, giving her all she asks for and more without requiring her to earn it. He does not discipline her or set any boundaries for her. He feeds off her being his star so he can play the role of the dedicated and doting father. As a result, she learns that she is the most important person to the exclusion of all others, including wives, girlfriends, and other siblings. She learns to control others, especially her dad, with her false charm and selfish temper.

Because she has never been disciplined, she lacks the ability to regulate her emotions. As an adult, she becomes a grown girl rather than a grown woman. Her father, on the other hand, gains his sense of identity through his image of being her dad. And both promote their unique relationship verbally, through pictures, bragging, social media, and any other way to show off their relationship. It is a symbiotic connection that does not allow either to mature or to expand in their individual lives. Neither becomes a wholly functioning person.

Power shift

By spoiling her, the father creates a monster. This type of father has a weak self-image so he pours all of himself into his daughter throughout her childhood. But when she becomes an adult, he loses control over her, and she begins dictating and running his life. She selfishly applies rules to him that she does not apply to herself. He is expected to be her doting assistant, where she can cancel plans on him even with short notice, while she would punish him for doing the same to her.

As adults, enmeshed fathers and daughters don't fight or disagree as healthy parents and their adult children do. These enmeshed relationships go beyond fighting and disagreeing; they break up. The adult child typically abandons or breaks up with her father until he acquiesces out of guilt and gives in to her demands. Their relationship has the dynamics of an unhealthy romantic relationship or marriage, where everything is based in intensity and fluctuates between love and hate. Whereas a healthy marriage is one that occurs between two equals, a daddy's girl relationship has no experience with equality when it comes to other people in her father's life, especially women. The daddy's girl sees herself as elevated and more special than all others in her father's life. When her father attempts to have a romantic relationship, she views her dad's affection for another woman as a demotion in her standings. She refuses to be treated as equal to another woman, and she resents feeling as if she has been topped by another woman in her father's life. For this reason, she will go to any end to destroy the relationships he tries to develop with women other than her. She will rage, abandon, and throw tantrums until she manipulates her way back into being her father's number one. Out of guilt, these types of fathers succumb to their daughters' obsessive, selfish demands. He has taught her how to prey upon his guilt, and she has learned her lesson well.

A power shift in the father/daughter relationship has occurred. She does not see her dad as a separate person with needs and desires of his own. She believes that his only desire should be for her. Anything less is intolerable.

Superficial identity

By spoiling his daughter, this type of father greatly interferes with her identity development. She does not know who she is if he is not constantly admiring her, aggrandizing her ego, and showing her off. He cripples her. She becomes unable to truly know her own thoughts, feelings, and opinions. She cannot tolerate boredom, being alone, or having to think deeply about anything in her life. If and when she is bored, she will call her dad and demand he come be with her. Entertaining herself is unthinkable. She acts in accordance with what he wants from her, often choosing career paths that guarantee his consistent admiration. She is only vested in keeping dad's attention, so she becomes exactly what he wants.

Because of this pattern, she becomes the consummate showoff. She is an obsessive self-promoter, constantly boasting about her achievements. She lives a parasitic life and thrives on provoking reactions in others to fuel her ego and sense of self. She uses everyone in her life to serve as a mirror for her specialness. Social media becomes her favorite place to promote herself, often having multiple accounts to court and grow her audience and demand that her dad promote her on his social media accounts. She is tragically empty and in need of being filled with compliments and adoration.

Emotionally unstable

Enmeshed daddy's girls live in a black-and-white world, judging everything superficially. Such a girl has been loved for her outer qualities and spoiled with gifts or accolades based in performance, causing her to develop very little depth concerning who she is. Because she has never had to face any real pain, out of her father's protection of her, she never develops the thought of the *other*. Therefore, she lacks empathy, maturity, and insight, which will later prove to be a real threat to her overall life satisfaction and happiness.

This deeply embedded insecurity causes her sense of self to fluctuate between extremes. For example, she feels either privileged or victimized, talented or worthless. She views herself as blessed or cursed. These fluctuations make her extremely moody, emotionally immature, and difficult to deal with. Sometimes these emotional opposites are felt every day and sometimes years apart, but for every privilege she receives from her father, there is a disgusted reaction from others.

Self-image problems

The enmeshed daddy's girl cannot hear about herself enough. She cannot feel herself unless she is being idolized. All conversations must be about her day, her mood, what so-and-so did or did not do for her, how life is unfair to her, and how great she is. And when things don't work out her way, she calls on dad to come rescue her from life's intolerances.

She tends to be heady and grandiose but with extreme low periods following because her father has completely curbed the development of her self-image. She is consistently needy and demanding of others, especially of her father, and has learned to show very little appreciation to others. These enmeshed daddy's girls have a higher likelihood of troubled relationships, depression, anxiety, addiction, and low self-esteem than many other girls do.

Covert erotica

When fathers spoil their daughters in this way, there is a certain erotica between them that is visible to those around them, and those who witness it usually have no idea how to talk about it or bring it up. Because there are no boundaries, these daughters are often found roaming around nearly naked in front of their father and any woman he may have in his life. This is just one of the ways they mark their territory and keep their dad's attention.

During a brief time, I dated a man with this toxic dynamic. His twenty-two-year-old daughter walked around in a bra and thong in front of him. She showered in his shower, napped in his bed, consistently ate the food off his plate, and groomed and dressed him as if she were his wife. It was absolutely mind-bending and ultimately creepy and sad. They had an extremely flirtatious relationship where she acted more like his romantic partner than his daughter. Anytime I spoke up out of shock, repulsion, and confusion, I was accused of being the "jealous girlfriend."

When fathers share this type of toxic dynamic with their child, their chances at having a lasting love or marriage outside of the one they already have with their toxic adult child is slim to none. These toxic adult children have no concern for the happiness or personal needs their parent may have. And these parents become too afraid to actively set healthier boundaries with their toxic adult children, which would help them learn to live a more normal lifestyle.

When parents hold the belief that their child is a superstar, these children are taught to believe the same about themselves, whether that's true in reality or not. As parents lavish their children with undue praise, their children fail to experience or learn to cope with the sting of constructive criticism that would make them well-rounded, empathic, and otherwise healthy people. The creation of this "special" life expectation is dangerous. These toxic adult children are raised to believe they are more unique than others, making them entitled to feel they can do whatever they like due to their special status in this world. The seeds of narcissism have been deeply embedded into their psyche—a self-perception their parents may eventually strive to fight against while their toxic adult children ignore them, refusing to see what they have become and are doing to themselves. Parents are left with no life aside from picking up the wreckage left by their toxic adult children.

I stopped dating the man I mentioned above, getting out of it for my own self-protection. This man's daughter was absolutely vicious and hell-bent on destroying any connection between us. This man came to understand that the dynamic he shared with his daughter was dysfunctional, but he was too afraid to set any limits with her.

My therapist helped me recognize that I was repeating in this relationship the toxic dynamic I grew up in with my family. This man's daughter was the golden child, my ex represented my toxic parents, and once again I was the scapegoat, the whistle-blower.

During my brief time in this dynamic, I continually questioned why and how I ended up in such a toxic relationship. What I finally learned was this. By our common human nature, we are all drawn to what is familiar. Consider. In my family triangle, my brother was the superstar athlete who went on to have a certain level of fame throughout his college and short professional athletic career. He was the adored, elevated, enmeshed golden child who could do no wrong. His standout athletic ability, good-boy charm, and fame were something my parents could readily feast off and use to put them in the spotlight for raising such a rare phenomenon. Likewise, my ex's daughter was an aspiring sports reporter who went to a well-known university to live the dream of one day becoming a famous woman sports reporter. Alongside her dad, they had dreams of her fame where he could proudly say he raised her on his own. I, however, was not the validated child in my family triangle irrespective of my more humble talents, gifts, or sensitive nature. And I was not the validated partner in the triangle between myself, my ex, and his daughter, regardless of my good heart, intelligence, success, and efforts of kindness toward her.

My personal notoriety as a nationally recognized expert with many television appearances, awards, and a large public following only made my ex's daughter more envious and her desire to get rid of me more intense. She told my ex the only reason I made it in my career is because of the size of my breasts and my blonde hair. She made it clear that when she makes it (which must mean on TV) that it will be due to her skill and talent. My ex did nothing to discipline or correct this disgusting declaration that she made about me. At the end of the day, my ex continually catered to his petulant, evil daughter so egregiously that he would regularly lie to me about their relationship and activities, offering a variety of reasons to cancel plans he and I had together. Then he would go out with his daughter, and she made sure to post pictures of them on social media so I would see who was in charge. Likewise, my parents have consistently chosen to heroize my brother and nearly completely ignore my day-to-day successes and the helpful and loving influence I've been able to have with so many people.

All of this is not about me feeling like a victim. It's about coming to understand the patterns I've repeated, resulting from being raised in a toxic family. I have used each painful relationship experience as a master teacher specifically designed for my healing. The only person I can save is myself. I am committed to diving deeply into examining why I do the things I do so I can stop repeating the same mistakes over and over again.

I am thankful to be a person who is compelled to understand herself.

I am thankful I am a person who will delve into what is deeply painful to find a way to repair it.

I am thankful to be a person who is unafraid to do whatever it takes to live and create a life of peace, healing, and happiness.

I am thankful for the mistakes I've made and every relationship I've had. It is because of these experiences that I have come to possess an increased sense of control and mastery over my life, as well as grown in wisdom regarding my decision-making and achieved a healthy self-esteem.

When we are raised in toxic families, we often go through a time period, and for some of us, a lifetime, of repeating the toxic patterns we were raised in with other people in our lives. We do this until we decide we've had enough pain and choose to genuinely examine our patterns and stop the craziness for good. It was my relationship with this enmeshed father that was my end point of repeating my childhood patterns. My short-term relationship with him and the dynamic of the toxic triangle I found myself in clearly brought to light the old pattern I was repeating. I could now begin to heal on a whole new level.

How to Parent Children to Become Healthy Adults

Healthy parents do not view their children as things, slaves, or psychological mirrors. Healthy parents view their children as growing and developing precious human beings. Children are loved with empathy and seen as sensitive, innocent, scared, elated, and curious about life. From the time children are very young, healthy parents are prepared for the fears in their children to be high and their self-esteem to be low, especially during certain phases of their life. For this reason, healthy parents remember from the day they conceive that their children are little people in need of their help, discipline, and guidance. Children need certain essentials to learn resilience, to love themselves, to care for others, to learn about failure, and to learn to turn their pain to the positive. To raise healthy children, parents need to be both tough and tender.

In an article I wrote for the *Huffington Post* in 2016, based on a list I saw created by Josh Shipp who is an expert on teenagers, I talked about the important messages our children need to hear from us to help them develop into exceptional, productive, and, most importantly, happy human beings. Here's what we parents need to do to raise our children to become healthy adults.

I love you

Parents can give their children too many things—clothes, toys, books, events, and the like. But parents can never give their children too much love. Telling our children we love them, and telling them often, lets them know they are precious to us. Hearing the words *I love you* gives our children the courage, verbal affirmation, and support they need. It provides them room to make mistakes. It provides healing and produces feelings of joy. We become a fan in their audience, but not gushing, doting fans who treat them as celebrities who can do no wrong. We are there for them, but in truly loving ways.

Think about it. How do children learn to love themselves? They learn to love themselves by how we love them as their parents. When we tell our children we love them, and we back that message with the actions to support it, we teach our children how to love themselves and how to love and be gracious toward others.

Healing Moment

Saying *I love you* takes away fear and provides our children with the confidence and security they need to sustain them throughout life.

I'm proud of you

In order to develop a healthy sense of self, children need a surplus of affirmation and validation. Children crave our support and blessings. The first people children think about impressing are always their parents. They direct the majority of their behaviors toward gaining our approval, love, and acceptance. Although many parents tell their children they are proud of them, the difference is made in the quality, quantity, and sincerity that we show them behind those words. Hugging, loving, and being present to our children are critical. Though as parents, we may not fully agree with the way our children choose to do some things, we must commend them on completing the hardest task of all—the journey into their independence.

I was wrong, I am sorry, you were right

We must be parents who are willing, open, and confident enough to admit to our children when we are wrong. When we do this, we show them we are human, that we are not perfect. We show them that we have compassion for how they feel on the other side of our mishaps. When we're real and self-effacing with our children, we show that perfection isn't possible, not for them and not for us. Accepting our own imperfections requires honesty. When we can take responsibility for our wrongs, we help our children accept and have the courage to examine and embrace their own imperfections. Being able to do this helps our children become balanced rather than perfectionistic. Taking ownership of our mistakes creates an environment of tolerance and open-mindedness, which later becomes the foundation upon which our children learn to build all of their future relationships.

I forgive you—you do not need to be perfect

We are all imperfect. There is no such thing as a perfect parent. We are guilty of saying things we don't mean and doing things we should not do. All of us waste time, break promises, forget important things, and mess up in countless other ways. None of us fully meets all the expectations placed upon us, including our own. We must keep this part of our humanity alive and in our minds when we parent our children so they too have room to be human. No one, no matter what age, appreciates being reminded of how they made a poor choice or mistake. Nor does anyone want to be punished endlessly for it, humiliated in front of others for it, or have it rubbed in their face. As parents, we have to find the balance between having our children face up to the consequences of their actions while remembering they have feelings too. It is our task to teach our children they are lovable despite their imperfections, discipline them appropriately, and forgive them when they go wrong.

I am here for you and listening

It is incredibly important to listen to our children so they know we are interested in what they have to say. Through listening we learn who our child is on the inside. It connects us to their inner world and creates an interaction that is mutually satisfying, where both parent and child feel a sense of value. To avoid needless misunderstandings, it is helpful to reflect back to our children what they have communicated as confirmation we have heard them correctly. Once understanding is established, we can encourage, guide, and praise them.

Negative bonds are created when a child feels unimportant. Being heard is a huge statement of worth. How can we know our children and be close to them if we never listen to them objectively? If we argue with them and consistently talk about our opinions, we are not listening. Our children are different than we are, so instead of telling them what to do and who to be all the time, we should be thoughtful to listen to them first, hear their thoughts, and then provide direction (if it is wanted), asking for their opinions and input. This helps our children learn to problem-solve, brainstorm, and make their own good decisions. Coming from a mother who only talked *at* me and told me what to do but very rarely listened to what I needed or felt, I cannot express how important it is for parents to listen.

This is your responsibility

Personal accountability is an important part of growing up. When our children make a decision—whether it is wise or not—dealing with the fallout of their decision goes along with training them. When parents make their children accountable, the result is effective lesson-learning. Our children will quickly learn which actions are positive and which produce negative results through having to take accountability. However, if we shame, humiliate, or fail to act with our children, we do not parent them to be responsible. The process of learning to make good decisions means our children will sometimes make poor decisions, and we need to let them make these choices. These experiences help them grow. We are there to teach, be involved when they need us, and guide them long into their future. When we hold our children accountable, we send the clear message that we believe in their abilities to do what they need to do. Without a deep understanding of responsibility, children never learn to lead their own lives effectively.

You have what it takes to succeed

The concept of success, being a direct result of effort and persistence, starts early. Healthy self-esteem is our child's protective armor against the challenges of the world. We must parent our children to know their strengths and weaknesses and to feel good about themselves. When we parent in this way, our children have an easier time handling conflicts and resisting negative pressures. When our children believe they have what it takes to succeed, they are generally more optimistic about life and what it has to offer them. One of the most valuable gifts we give our children is our belief in them. We must reward and celebrate their efforts and achievements and support them when they fail. We must teach them that failure is a necessary part of life and something that helps train them to succeed. Failures teach our children to discover the missing pieces in the plan they had so they can develop those pieces and try again. As our children learn to triumph through their failures, they will pave their way to living a happy and fulfilling life.

We must allow love and discipline to be the guiding forces of our parenting. Discipline and humiliation are different. If we crush the self-esteem of our children at any age, the effects are lifelong. Be mindful because once our children reach adulthood, it's harder to make changes in how they see and define themselves. For this reason, it is wise to think about developing and promoting self-esteem as early as possible, with consistency and authenticity. As our children try, fail, try again, fail again, and finally succeed, they develop ideas about what their capabilities are. At the same time, they are also building ideas about themselves based upon the interactions they are having with us and others. The more supportive and positive these interactions are, the more resilient and self-confident our children become.

Healing Moment

 It is our love and discipline that guide our children into forming accurate and healthy ideas of who they are.

Lyric Therapy
I hope you're somewhere prayin', prayin'
I hope your soul is changin', changin'
I hope you find your peace
Falling on your knees, prayin'
—"Praying," by Kesha[17]

6

Toxic Siblings, Grandparents, and In-Laws

Toxicity exists in every area and in every layer of a toxic family. Toxic doesn't leave out anyone regardless of their title or role in your life. As we've been learning, our parents can be toxic, our children can be toxic, and so can our siblings, in-laws, and grandparents. Some of us may even have pets that are toxic (just kidding). As we learn about toxic people, our learning must be directed toward changing our minds about our toxic family members and opening our minds to the idea that toxicity exists anywhere that a person's character is destructively flawed, even in a grandmother.

Toxic Siblings

When we have toxic siblings, it's painful. We find it hard to live a life next to a toxic sibling who always needs to keep us at arm's length or who is only kind to us when he or she stands to benefit. Toxic sibling relationships are almost always created by the parents through the scapegoat and golden child dynamics.

In an article written by Carolyn Steber on a website called Bustle,[18] she teaches that anyone with a sibling understands that tiffs, quarrels, blowout disagreements, and even the occasional pinch, slap, or hair-pull are healthy and to be expected. These squabbles are usually resolved, and as siblings mature, they cease to exist. If the family dynamics are healthy and sibling closeness is encouraged, the connection between siblings generally improves by the time they reach adulthood. Unfortunately, a significant number of adults have conflictual relationships with their siblings, and many, like myself, have no relationship with them at all. Many siblings dismiss the hostilities that exist between them as normal. It is easy for us to dismiss the tensions we experience with our siblings for quite some time until they begin crossing over into toxic territory. Steber gives us some clues as to when the relationships we have with our siblings turn toxic.

They only contact you when they need something

When our siblings only call us because they need something, they see us as something to use rather than as persons worth connecting with.

It is normal for siblings to experience a passage of time where they grow apart in young to mid adulthood. During this time, each sibling is growing in their independence, defining their identities through love relationships, perhaps attending college, and starting career paths. As adults, we begin to share commonalities, such as marriage, having children, and stable careers. We have more time for family. This is often when healthy siblings get back in touch and begin sharing experiences together.

However, if our relationship is still toxic and the only time our sibling contacts us is because he or she needs or wants something from us, the relationship is not reciprocal but rather one-sided.

You dread seeing them

Even though most of us only have to see our siblings a few times a year, the dread of seeing them at all can still be present. If the thought of seeing our sibling puts a knot of anxiety in our stomach, then we are likely preparing ourselves to be around someone who is overtly or covertly mean or selfish. Maybe it feels like our sibling has to outshine us, or he has to disparage us to make himself feel better, or maybe he even offers us help in some way as a way to indicate that we're below him. Whatever the pattern is, we want to avoid it because of the constant anxiety we feel when around that toxic brother or sister. We could boil this down to our own insecurity, but usually if we dread only being around specific people, it's because they are huge contributors to making us feel insecure, repulsed, fearful, or anxious.

They are manipulative

Even in adulthood, healthy siblings will occasionally have their arguments, and each will take some responsibility in them. However, if our sibling is constantly starting arguments and throwing the blame back onto us, she is manipulating. These types of siblings enjoy creating an imbalance of power as a method to exploit us and get what they want.

They consistently disparage you

For the golden child sibling, it is usually not enough to have been the superstar of our family where everything has worked smoothly for her the majority of the time. Our golden child sibling has to continually make sure we know of her superior status to ours. It's not unusual for siblings to belittle each other under the guise of playful banter since teasing is a common family dynamic, but a sibling who constantly leaves us feeling in the one-down position is likely toxic.

If we're not sure if our sibling means well and just sometimes takes it too far, we must consider how often we end up feeling hurt while in their presence. A healthy sibling relationship should be fairly equal. Everyone will make mistakes from time to time and hurt the other person, but these situations shouldn't be skewed toward only one person. Toxic siblings don't just tease but demean. They seek to elevate themselves at all costs, leaving us feeling responsible and inferior.

They are abusive

It's never okay for a person to abuse us, but that doesn't stop a lot of people from assuming it's normal for sibling fights to occasionally become hostile. However, if our adult sibling is harmful emotionally or verbally, it can quickly escalate into a bigger problem that can turn physical if no one is there to intervene.

They try to ruin your relationship with other family members

Toxic family members enjoy stirring the pot. It's not uncommon for toxic family members to agitate in order to get people to turn on each other. Call it a love for drama or just downright insane. Either way we look at it, the golden child has to make sure the scapegoat stays in the scapegoated position. If the scapegoat does anything to succeed or stand out, the golden child will make sure to steal the show by putting other family members in the middle to make the scapegoat appear to be the person at fault. My brother did this to me, not just with my parents. He used me to cover for lies in his personal life. Any way he could use me to throw me under the bus to help him escape wrong as an adult, he did so without shame, setting me up to face the consequences of his lies while having to explain myself.

Toxic Grandparents

Make no mistake: there are toxic grandparents out there. Any of us who have had in-laws or toxic parents, which has been a large number of us, know without a doubt that grandparents can be toxic. If our parents were toxic to us, why would they be any less toxic and dangerous to our children and spouses?

Healing Moment

 Manipulators manipulate everyone all the time.

Toxic grandparents will quickly grab the new grandparent identity joyously when they're around our children. However, a new title doesn't create a new person. Toxic grandparents have very little desire to take too much of a roll in the lives of their grandchildren. They view their grandchildren as means to meet their own needs just as they viewed us when we were children. Or, on the other extreme, if our toxic parents were enmeshed, they will not just want to babysit our children; they will take over the parenting of them, creating in us the feeling that we are second to our parents in the eyes of our children.

My mother made it clear to me that she was *not* going to be the type of grandmother who babysat all the time or have the kids overnight because this would interfere with her own routine. My daughter and I did not see her more than twice a year and for less than one week each trip. And yet my mother became convinced that my daughter was in some type of unusually deep bond with her boyfriend, and she made it sarcastically clear to me that she was not my daughter's favorite. My mother created this same story with another grandchild in our family, and she became utterly offended when this grandchild wouldn't talk to her or acknowledge her. She complained that he was mean and ignored her. The truth is that this child was shy and more introverted. His behavior had nothing to do with my mother. But, of course, in her eyes, it did. For a very long time my mother had nothing pleasant to say about this grandchild until he aged some, grew out of his shyness, and finally started to give her the attention she required. Now she "loves" him because *he* makes *her* feel good, which is not his responsibility.

The most dangerous thing about toxic grandparents is they have no problem driving a wedge between us and our children. My mother was more than willing to develop a relationship with my ex-husband even though she had refused to speak to him for eleven years. This confused me since she was aware of how neglectful and irresponsible he was then and still is. During the years we've been divorced, my mother has suggested I report him to child protective services for his lack of appropriate cleanliness. She also had multiple conversations with me about creating a living will to make sure that if I were to pass away, none of my assets or life insurance policies would ever go to him. She would go on and on about how he would spend all the money and my daughter would see none of it. She suggested I make her the executor of my money and assets in case I died. Now, however, she shamelessly tries to develop a relationship with him so she can see my daughter behind my back and without my permission. Not only does this triangulate my daughter between myself and my mother, but it places a toxic dynamic between my daughter and my ex-husband, and my ex-husband and myself. The hurt and shock my daughter felt knowing my mother was doing this generated fear and anger in her.

Healing Moment

 Our children should never feel put in the middle against the one parent or parents who raise them.

The most important thing we do for our children is teach them right from wrong. Sadly, when we have toxic parents, we have to teach our children the difference between love and manipulation long before we want to.

The most important thing our children need is for us to be happy and whole. Our children do not need or require a relationship with their grandparents to be that way, but they need us, as their parents, to be happy, functioning, and complete. If we need to set firm boundaries on our toxic parents to attain high levels of emotional and mental health, then we are doing the right thing for our whole family.

Toxic In-Laws

When our parents are toxic, we can bet they will bring their toxicity into every area of our lives, and that includes our marriage. Because they thrive on the divide-and-conquer technique, they can easily turn our spouse into the scapegoat or targeted family member. Shannon Thomas explains that our toxic family members do all they can to block our spouse from feeling any sense of inclusion into our family. Their goal is to make our spouse feel rejected, unwanted, disliked, unwelcomed, and pushed out.

One of my male patients whose mother-in-law is toxic struggles in this exact way. His mother-in-law makes sure to leave him out in every way possible. If she sees his photos on Facebook, she will only make comments on his wife and their kids, acting as if my patient doesn't exist and wasn't even in the photo. In another move to drive a wedge between my patient and his wife, his mother-in-law un-followed him on Facebook and had all her siblings un-follow him as well. I helped this couple set clear and firm limits on the amount of time this toxic mother-in-law spends with them and on what they are and are not willing to tolerate when it comes to her behavior. This puts tension between my patient's wife and her mother, but his wife understands these boundaries are necessary for the health of her marriage.

When our spouse complains to us about the poor treatment our toxic parents act out on them, our toxic parents will accuse our spouse of being too sensitive and making up things. In fact, they will pull out the manipulative techniques of projection and deflection and accuse our spouse of leaving *them* out, of making *them* feel unwelcomed, thereby scapegoating our spouse for all of their own behaviors. The minute we stand up for our spouse, we are accused of taking their side, of not believing our toxic parents as they try to manipulate us into believing our spouse is now turning us against them. This type of chaos is exactly what our toxic parents strive for. There are times when our toxic parents will threaten and follow through on abandoning us if we don't leave our spouse. A father of a patient of mine did this to him. He put my patient in a position to have to choose between having him in his life or staying in his marriage with his wife and children. My patient chose to forgo a relationship with his toxic father and to stay happily married to his wife. When my patient chose his family over his father, his father refused to speak to him for two years. Since that time, my patient's father continues to stir up gossip and throws out covert threats around my patient's wife.

On the other side of this well-known dynamic, there are toxic in-laws who try to get our own spouse to turn against us by taking their side in a conflict. Our toxic parents will prey upon our spouse in an effort to break down any of the boundaries we've set on them around our children, our needs for personal freedom, and other issues such as finances. Toxic parents, depending on their unique agenda, either view our spouse as the enemy they need to get rid of to get back into their desired position of power, or they see our spouse as the person to triangulate against us. Their goal is to overcome and even decimate the boundaries we have placed on them.

No matter the dynamic, it is common for toxic people to silence or smear anyone who has the courage to stand up to their manipulation. There is a real difference between a person who may not agree with our choices and who backs away to give us the space to learn on our own and the toxic person who completely ostracizes us for going against what he or she thinks is right or correct. Each of us must take ownership over our lives and the needs we have for those critical optimal frustration experiences necessary for our personal growth and development. Healthy people offer this time and space. Toxic people, on the other hand, cut us off or try to destroy us, our relationships, and our reputation as ways to stifle our independence.

Lyric Therapy
You could never know what it's like
Your blood like winter freezes just like ice
And there's a cold lonely light that shines from you
You'll wind up like the wreck you hide behind that mask you use
—"I'm Still Standing," by Elton John[19]

7

You're Not Crazy

One strong indicator that we have been raised in a toxic family is our feeling plagued with consistent feelings of doubt and confusion. As children, we are preprogrammed at our very core to believe in and follow our parents. This belief is hardwired into us by biology and evolution and it is not under our control. The reason is because the children who believed their parents' words and direction were less vulnerable to danger. When our parents genuinely love us, their words are well-meaning, they tell the truth, and they strive to protect us. However, this dynamic fails when parents are manipulating their children and lying to them, focused on protecting their own self-image or fragile ego rather than their children. Those persons given to us to help us survive and thrive work to only use us, hurt us, deceive us, and break us—all for their demented, twisted purposes. As their children, we want to believe them and follow them as we're hardwired to do, but they use what was meant for our good against us.

Abusers use confusion as a key manipulative technique to keep their children off balance. There is no security in a world where we are raised to not even trust our own perceptions. How do we know what reality really is if we cannot judge it correctly? This is how and why we come to believe we must be the one in the dynamic who is crazy. It is these feelings of confusion that keep us from seeing reality. The more confused and off balance our toxic parents keep us, the more insecure we get, the needier we become, and the more we seek them to feel a sense of security and sanity. This is what our toxic parents count on. This is how they keep us in the one-down position. The more confused we are, the less power we have because we are unable to think rationally. The human psyche doesn't function well in uncertainty. When we grow up in these types of dynamics, it deeply damages our ability to distinguish if other relationships we have are healthy or toxic.

When our feelings of anxiety are chronic and not transient, we need to pay attention. If we live in chronic stress in a relationship and we never know where we stand, something is wrong. Healthy relationships do not persistently pull us into these types of negative emotional states.

Healing Moment

 Toxic people don't love—they manipulate.

Children who are raised by these types of parents live from a wounded, false, but deeply held belief that they are inherently flawed. We are taught to think there is some mystery flaw in us that is so hideous that no one could ever love us. The sad part is that the "flawed and hideous" thing about us is something we have no clarity on. We cannot figure out what it is to even fix it, cure it, or prevent it. This mystery awful thing about us is just there and not under our control or direction; therefore, we cannot even hide it. We are raised to believe that whatever this "badness" is, it is not something we do but *who we are*. This causes us to live with an all-encompassing sense of shame. I remember after experiencing a devastating breakup, I asked my mother, "Why am I not lovable?" With annoyance in her voice, she said, "Why do you always ask that?" The reason is no mystery. My toxic parents taught me that I wasn't lovable because I was seriously flawed.

Toxic parents essentially brainwash us into believing we are fundamentally unlikable, which leaves us terrified throughout our lives that other people are going to discover our mysterious flaw and decide to end their relationship with us. We learn to live our lives pleasing others or not interacting at all as a way to avoid risking ever being found out and abandoned. To survive in our family, we had to become an inauthentic version of ourselves to try to fit into the fakeness of the family dynamic. And we continue to do this even outside the family. We live inauthentic lives, and we do this without even knowing why, without really understanding what we are doing.

Over much time, self-examination, reading, journaling, and weekly therapy, I have come to discover what is so awful and hideous about me. It is not a mystery to me anymore. This "awful," "unlovable," "repulsive" thing about me is that I have *needs* of my own—a truly normal human condition. Our toxic family members do not like anyone who has their own needs because they only view others as sources for meeting *their* needs. Needing time, love, and attention from my toxic family members made me difficult, hard to love, annoying, guilty, and angry. I have had to learn as an adult that having needs doesn't make me needy. I have had to learn that having personal needs of my own in a relationship should not cause anyone to find me repulsive, a burden, or someone who asks for too much.

Healing Moment

 We should not have to be needless for someone to love us.

Why Do We Keep Going Back?

It's hard to understand that when we know our family members are out to intentionally hurt us, why we just can't get away and stay away. Two deeply fundamental things keep us going back to our toxic family members.

First, they are our family. Who doesn't want to be connected to their family? These are the people we are supposed to be connected to and spend our lives sharing memories with. For this reason, we keep trying and trying to stay connected to them, only to find that we continue to come to the same conclusion: we're not emotionally safe with them.

The second thing that keeps us going back to our toxic family members is the need for closure. If we're going to part ways, we want to do it with a healthy sense of closure. Because toxic people know we desire to be in the truth, that we desire to have all parties on the same page after a disagreement, closure is the one thing our toxic family members will never give us, at least not intentionally. To toxic people, giving us closure is the same as admitting wrong, and this is not something they will ever do.

After my disastrous birthday with my toxic family, I didn't have contact with my mother for almost two months, but an unexpected tragedy happened in my personal life which left me so devastated and feeling alone that I called her. I remember her saying, "I thought I was never going to hear from you again." She made it very clear to me, in that moment, that had I not reached out to her, she never ever would have reached out to me.

Healing Moment

If they couldn't give you love, don't look to them for closure. Lock that door and move on.

—*John Mark Green*

The hardest part about leaving toxic family members is the fact that we leave denied of our own experience because they will never admit they have wronged us. They will go to their death denying the severity of our experience. This denial makes it harder for us and our recovery. When we grow up in all of these mixed messages, we end up feeling guilty and horrible for the lack of parental love we never received. When we blame ourselves for this lack, we carry *their* shame. We have to shoulder all of their dysfunction on our own. We suffer while our toxic family members act above reproach for the suffering they've caused. How is this fair or right? It is neither, and deep inside of us we know this. Still, we stay connected to them as children because we have no other choice. As children we need them for food, home, and shelter. As adults, on the other hand, we have choice, but we are often too afraid to think of life without them because they are our parents and they feel necessary to have in our lives. It's hard to imagine life without parents, no matter what age we are. We need to believe our toxic parents are good. We reason that if they are good, then we are the ones who have to be bad and responsible for the problems in the relationship, which is why we keep going back and making efforts to repair things while they do nothing.

I have come to believe that toxic parents never wanted adult children. Instead they wanted dependent infants. The most effective way they could keep us in an infantile and non-functioning space was to make us feel too broken to ever leave them. If we are broken, we will need them always, and they will use their counterfeit kindness to keep us coming back after we think we've finally decided that we've tolerated enough of their abuse. Going back again and again is the hardest obstacle to overcome when it comes to toxic family relationships. After all, none of us want to be family-less. We go back because we love and want to feel loved. We are healthy enough to love and to know that we need to be loved in return. Because of our parents' doses of well-orchestrated moments of intermittent kindness, we get confused. We appear to see they have "good" in them, but we must come to see that this is just a façade.

Healing Moment

 This pattern of "come here, go away" is constant in toxic family ties.

The come-here, go-away pattern is not love. We must ask ourselves, Do we only want to feel good sometimes and to live a life chronically questioning where we stand? Do we want to live a life terrified of when the bottom will once again unexpectedly fall out? If we don't want to live this way, we have to get out.

Tina Fuller, author of *It's My Turn*, teaches that our anxiety can be a direct result of our parent's manipulative behavior. Though high anxiety also has genetic implications, children are more likely to be anxious if their parents openly criticize them, doubt their abilities, threaten to abandon them, are controlling, or are emotionally cold to the point that psychologists can predict a parent's behavior before ever observing it. This is because toxic people create a special kind of situational anxiety that is very different than organic, or biologically rooted, anxiety. Situational anxiety that comes from our toxic family members goes to the core of our self-esteem and our sense of personal value, which morphs into a lack of self-trust and a deep fear of people. With organic anxiety, it doesn't always have such a specific focus; rather, the anxiety seems to come on out of nowhere and that is what a person becomes the most afraid of—of not being able to control their anxiety.

Toxic parents make it a game to withhold love and approval just to see us chase them for it. Withholding what we need to feel loved and secure gives them power because it keeps us needing them and focused on them, which is exactly what they want. They enjoy the game of keeping us making efforts toward them while they continue to move the goal post so we can't ever score. It is the classic no-win love game. But as children, how could we have known what they were up to?

Because toxic family members feel an entitlement to us and they hate losing someone to pick on, they have a pattern of continually coming back through hovering (see chapter 9). This means that for any change in the dysfunctional relationship to occur, the pressure is on us to change our pattern of letting them seep back into our lives. We have to change our pattern to one of strict and unbendable boundaries no matter how seductive their ploys are to suck us back in. We must use our wisdom as gleaned from many years of experience. The greatest joy a toxic person has is the game of losing us and trying to seduce us back.

Why give them this type of power?

How do we make them better or healthier people by giving in to them?

And what about us? Don't we show how little we matter to ourselves if we succumb to them—yet again?

Asking these questions and honestly answering them are where our healing begins.

Healing Moment

Every time we go back to toxic relationships, we're reopening a wound that was in the process of healing.

Danu Morrigan, the daughter of a narcissistic mother, believes that we feel obligated to return to our parents partly because we're trying to make sense of the fact that our own family, especially our mother, does not truly love us. In a child's logic, our parents are flawless, so if they don't love us, there must be a defect in us, not in them.

In my own therapy, my therapist said to me that as long as I believe that I am the problem, I will harbor a hope that things in the relationship with my toxic family members can change because I have the power to change myself. We erroneously believe that if we try to be good enough, successful, or perfect, maybe our toxic family members will change their minds about us. But they don't and they won't.

Now if the problem isn't within us, then that creates a horribly scary feeling. That means we're powerless to make any positive changes in how our toxic family members treat us. I certainly know that I can do nothing to change anything in myself that would ever make a difference in my relationships with my family members. At one time, this rocked my world. But now, I just feel relief. I am no longer brainwashed by them into believing that I am the bad kid, the problem child, the difficult one. I know the truth about my family and have accepted it.

Healing Moment

The only reason I am difficult for my parents is precisely because I am *not* toxic.

Let me reassure you of the following:

- You're not crazy.
- You're not fundamentally flawed.

- There is nothing inherently awful about you.
- You *are* lovable, but your parents were not and are not love-*able*. They are incapable of giving you love.

The only closure we need, and the only closure we will ever get, will have to come from within us. It comes at that defining moment when something changes in our heart. When we finally reach our capacity. The last pebble of pain they add to an already full-beyond-capacity bag of rocks is the transgression that finally causes the bag to burst open. In my case, the last pebble wasn't my most painful experience with my toxic family members, but it had just enough weight to tear apart the bag. Toxic people never want to focus on all the rocks they've added to that bag over our lifetime that represent their patterns of toxic behavior. They only want to focus on the most recent transgression. So they act as if they are utterly shocked when we finally reach our limit. They claim that what they did to us wasn't a big enough deal for us to reach any healthy limit with them inside of ourselves. When we point out that damaging rocks have spilled all over the floor, they accuse us of never letting go of the past and holding grudges, although they have never taken any accountability for the mass destruction they have added to our bag.

The rip in the fabric of the load we carry, as painful as it feels, is actually a blessing. It signals that our healing can now begin. Our toxic family members finally did something that made us hit our place of enough. We're finally done taking their abuse.

Do They Ever Change?

We all want to believe that our toxic family members can change. We have experienced that our toxic family members have sides of them that seem good. But these good sides are bait. They are used to cover-up who they really are so they can continue to manipulate us. Our toxic family members respond to relationships in these ways because they lack character. As unbelievable and painful as this is to hear, our toxic family members do not care about how what they do impacts us as long as what they're doing feeds their ego.

Our toxic family members would rather go to their grave than to admit wrong.

Not one of us is perfect. We all have our flaws. But when we are healthy, even if we're sometimes selfish and work hard to be more unselfish, this effort and insight alone makes us a drastically different person than someone who is truly toxic. It's so hard for a healthy person to grasp that toxic people have zero insight. If our toxic family members seem to have glimpses or moments of insight, they do not inspire them enough to want to put any effort into changing their ways. They don't value other people enough to change. The only needs that make sense to them are the needs they have for themselves, and they will do the most vile things to the people they love (their own children, grandchildren, or siblings) to get those needs met.

To make matters worse, our toxic family members hold a nearly squeaky clean outward image. They are completely dedicated to preserving an image of perfection. I liken them to billboards. They are careful to maintain an image and reputation of moral purity, and they worry a great deal about what other people think about them. My mother has run many charity events in my brother's name to raise money for her ski camps, and she now teaches suicide classes at the high school. She had the gall to say to me one day, "Did you know the number one reason teenagers commit suicide? It is due to divorce." I looked at her in disbelief. After her almost four marriages, she couldn't relate that statistic as relevant to me or any of the suffering I went through as she selfishly kept moving from one relationship to the next. She was intentional in telling me that statistic to simply be cruel and invalidating, but she slyly delivered it as if this was a shocking fact.

Psychiatrist Scott Peck teaches that the only thing our toxic family members hold concern for is their outward image. Although they seem to lack the desire to be good, they are intensely driven to appear good. Our toxic family members are committed to being viewed as altruistic and innocent. They go to work and are well dressed, superficially polite, and pleasing. Because they look good, we begin to think we're making things up about them, that they can't really be as insensitive to us as they really are. But their goodness in essence is a lie. This lie isn't necessarily created to deceive others but so they can avoid the reality of who they really are. Our toxic family members absolutely refuse to tolerate the pain that would come from their own self-examination, even assuming they would conduct it honestly and deeply. Peck says that people only lie when they're attempting to cover-up something. Our toxic family members cannot stand to look into the negative mirror of who they really are, so they continue to lie and decorate the billboard of their false image to keep them away from the ugly truth. They do this by projecting out to others that everyone else is fake, bad, and ugly. The reality, however, is that those traits belong to them.

No, we are *not* crazy. Our toxic family members genuinely are as displeasing, horrible, exhausting, and painful to be around as we experience them to be. Period. We need to pay attention not to what they look like on the outside but how we feel around them on the inside.

The Toxic Roller Coaster

Anyone who can watch us cry and break under the cruelty of their actions and do nothing to change their ways after that is not a loving or healthy person. Toxic family members desire to sit front row in the audience of our suffering and bear witness to the pain they have caused us. Our toxic family members are notorious for living by unequal rules. They expect us to tolerate abuses from them that they would never tolerate from someone else. They create rules for us that they do not follow or subscribe to. Our toxic family members will make ridiculous and unreasonable demands of us and expect our complete loyalty, respect, and unconditional love at all times. Meanwhile, they keep breaking these same rules and are not at all capable of giving anything of themselves to us in return. We end up living a life of walking on eggshells while they are out perusing around being disloyal, disrespectful, and unloving.

It doesn't matter how well we do, how loving we are, or how much we give, do, or have. None of it will ever be enough for a toxic person. Instead we become like Gumby. We bend and flex and bend and flex, all to no avail. Our toxic family members are totally unable to act with reason. They are so needy that they cannot be filled no matter how much we give out. We are like hamsters on a wheel. We work hard and run fast but fail to get anywhere with our destructive family. This is how life will forever be with them, because *our toxic family members will not change.* They love the power of making us feel as if we are not enough. They find things wrong with us where there is nothing wrong with who we are, what we do, or how we treat them.

They eventually drive us to shutdown—the point at which we come to feel nothing for them. We look at them and see people we cannot stand and would prefer to get away from.

The healthiest thing we can do for ourselves is to get away and cease all efforts at trying to please them. If they are incapable of doing for themselves what they demand we do for them, the greatest gift we give to them is to let go so they can try to figure it out on their own. But figure it out, they won't. Rather, they will find another person to prey on.

Follow Your Gut

Our gut instincts are rarely crazy. They exist by design to support our ability to survive and thrive. If something in the way our family members treat us doesn't feel right and hits us hard in the gut, we must start to trust our own sense of what's real and follow our own instincts. We often ignore our gut instincts around the red flags in our relationships because we don't want to see them. We don't want to look at a reality that may veer largely from our dream. We don't want to look at them because … they hurt.

Healing Moment

 The longer we ignore red flags, pretend they don't exist, the more we disconnect from ourselves.

Why do we do this?

Because we want to love and be loved by the family we were raised in, and we erroneously believe that one day they will wake up and be different. Unfortunately, our toxic family members will most often not change for the better but will likely change for the worse. Paying attention to those red flags may place us in a position to make a painful decision, but this decision will save our lives and our mental and emotional wellness long-term. It's excruciating when the red flags are there and we don't want them to be. However, if we can acknowledge them, we will save ourselves years of pain.

We must take responsibility to be loving toward ourselves, especially if we're unable to receive love from the people who have raised us. We must give ourselves a break and be compassionate toward ourselves. We must acknowledge that it is natural to feel completely crazy around our toxic family members.

Shannon Thomas lets us know that when we are first beginning to recognize that someone is toxic, we often describe that person as being "nice at times," or we say that he or she has "good moments." As healthy people, we interpret these moments of kindness to be reflective of their overall character, and we start blaming ourselves or other external situations for the more rampant manipulative behavior of these individuals.

Why?

Because we love them, and we want to believe they are good people.

Sadly, it is this way of thinking that keeps us confused. It severs us from reality.

Thomas teaches that a toxic person isn't a loving person with a cruel side that shows up once in a while. Rather, our toxic family members *are* the cruel side of themselves, and they work assiduously to disguise themselves as the "nice person" only when it suits them, such as when they need something or when they sense they've pushed us too far. The hard thing is that when they show us kindness, it is such a relief that this feigned kindness becomes embellished in our own experience. We feel their kindness to be more genuine than it really is. If we categorize our toxic family members in this way, we cannot see them as a whole. We must see them as they really are. The very large majority of the time, our toxic family members are harmful people, telling us that *we* are what cause them to act in the cruel ways they do.

We deserve better than what they dish out to us.

Lyric Therapy

You belong among the wildflowers
You belong in a boat out at sea
You belong with your love on your arm
You belong somewhere you feel free
—"Wildflowers," by Tom Petty[20]

8

No Contact

What we face when living in toxic family dynamics is the harsh reality that not all things are meant to work out. Some relationships are not meant to be ours. There are going to be those who say they love us but who also show an absolute refusal to take our heart into consideration. How can that be love? We must come to accept the fact that someone saying they love us and someone actually loving us are drastically different.

When we talk about letting go of or separating from our toxic family members, we are not doing so to be mean or cruel or unkind. We are not doing so to be unloving. The only way our toxic family members have any shot at changing for the better is to give them the correct or natural consequences for their own behavior and poor treatment of us. When someone does terrible things to us and experience no consequences coming back on them, we enable them to continue in their destructive ways and even contribute to making them into worse versions of who they already are.

Healing Moment

Enabling is not loving. Cutting ties is not cruelty.

We have every right to distance ourselves from people who have no other intention toward us other than controlling us, cutting us down, or otherwise putting us into states of horrible emotional pain and confusion. Cutting ties with them is not only self-loving but also the most loving thing we can do for them. If our toxic family members treat us terribly, then it is logical and just that they don't deserve to have us in their lives. Whether our toxic family members take the opportunity to learn, repent, humble themselves, change, or apologize is not for us to worry about. We need to start showing a deep and loving concern for ourselves in the ways our toxic family members never did. I have learned through my experience that sometimes the best way to love certain individuals is to leave them to keep company with themselves.

Knowing when to let go is incredibly important. It is amazing how many of us hang on to something we know we'd be better off releasing from our grasp. We act as if we're afraid to lose what we don't even have. We convince ourselves that it's better to have something than it is to have nothing. The reality is that to have anything halfway brings us more pain than it does to have nothing at all. When we have something halfway, it is like trying to navigate a stop sign and go sign at the same time. We can't go and we can't stop, so we're stuck. Whenever we have something halfway, it only keeps us hoping that if we hang in there long enough, maybe one day we will get the whole package. We live in the world of Maybe One Day.

The halfway world, however, is not a loving world, a validating world, or a world where we will ever feel loved or significant. We will always feel less than, not worthy. We will have to constantly audition to get our halfway toxic family members to love us, and this they will not do. We have to work against our feelings of poor self-worth and the deep belief that everyone will eventually come to see us as "in the way."

While none of this expresses the truth about us, for us to see and experience who we really are, we must let go of the toxic relationships that hold us down and convince us that we are unworthy and unlovable.

Options

When it comes to letting go of relationships with our toxic family members, we have some options available to us. I know from experience and from treating others that it is essential to try all of these options. When we try everything, it makes our final decision to go no contact more comfortable as we come to see the toxic people in our lives leave us with no other choice.

The first step to setting limits on these toxic relationships is the option of *cordial contact*. Through this option, we *fake it 'til we make it* when in the presence of our toxic family members. With cordial contact we are mindful not to be too self-revealing. We make sure to keep conversations and emotions superficial, positive, and pleasant, and largely about our toxic family members. Because they love feeling as if everything is about them, we can use this as a workable strategy, knowing we're doing it on purpose as a way to keep ourselves safe from unwanted drama, at least to the best of our ability. Knowing we're doing this on purpose helps us to avoid beating ourselves up for always acquiescing our needs to our toxic family members as a way to make them happy. Cordial contact can work, at least in the short-term. The problem is that our manipulative family members do not like it when things are peaceful or cordial, so they are likely to get under our skin in one way or another, striving to cause us to lose control of our objective and end up back in their web of destruction.

Another option is initiating a relationship of *low contact* with our toxic family members. In this option, we choose only to see or talk to them at family gatherings or other major holidays or events. Outside of this, we do all we can to avoid them. This option also may work for a while, but our toxic family members will catch on quickly and do all they can to force their way fully back into our lives.

I tried both of these options with my toxic family members, and as long as we weren't living in the same state, it worked. But the minute we would be together in person, their manipulations would begin, and before I knew it, I would be defending myself, and they would be acting as if I were the worst, most horrid human being to ever exist.

Healing Moment

When we pull back, our toxic family members will become more demanding and outrageous in their behavior. They will escalate even the smallest disagreements into full-blown battles to make sure we are left feeling as if we are the bad person in the mix.

The bottom line is this. When our toxic family members sense we've pulled away or are pulling back, they escalate their manipulations because they do not respect any of our needs for space. They do not want us having the space or time to think rationally about our relationship with them, because once we do, they get exposed and lose. For this reason, the middle ground is the worst place to be with our toxic family members. They have no idea how to function in that arena. They prefer to be all in or all out. When our toxic family members feel the gray area between us, what they usually do is cut ties with us.

The final incident that led to my complete break with my mother concerned a white car and a restaurant. Rather than follow my daughter and me in our white car to the designated restaurant, my mother and her current boyfriend accidentally followed the wrong car and ended up in the wrong place. I saw the mistake they made and tried calling them four times in less than two miles to help them navigate their way to the right restaurant. But they chose not to answer their phones. The boyfriend is as pathologically toxic as my mother. Once they arrived at the correct restaurant, he called me "a disrespectful, insolent person" in front of my daughter. Neither mentioned my attempts to reach them. And my mother, who complains incessantly about how this man emotionally abuses and bullies her, did not stand up for me when he was attacking me.

When I stood up for myself and set my boundaries, my mother and her boyfriend decided to leave the restaurant. She hugged me goodbye and indicated to me that her boyfriend was acting ridiculous, but because she chooses men over her children, she quit speaking to me. She also didn't text me goodbye in the morning before their flight took off like she normally does, but she did text my daughter goodbye that morning. I then found out a week later, after hearing nothing from her, that she and her boyfriend had already reached out to my ex-husband and to our close family friend from home and started their smear campaign against me. To this day my mother goes around and lies, telling everyone that I cut her off from being able to get in contact with me and my daughter by phone and email.

What I did as a result of this moment of abuse and abandonment and with the knowledge that she was smearing me to those closest to me was to refuse to defend myself or try to smooth things over with her. I made the firm decision to stop trying to mend fences with her anymore. It seemed best for me to leave her alone and simply do nothing further. After a month or so of no contact from her and still hearing about her smear campaign from people back home and watching the texts and videos she was sending to my daughter, which was something she had never done prior to this event, I made the decision to block her access to me to protect myself and my family. I put into effect the no-contact option.

Healing Moment

To toxic people, one person dumping or abandoning another person is the only choice because actually changing their behavior in order to preserve and keep a relationship with us is never an option.

The No-Contact Option

When we finally reach the point with our toxic family members where we decide the only healthy option for us is to go *no contact*, we have arrived on the frontlines of a very challenging, freeing, and yet deeply painful decision. If we are at this place, we can trust that we more than likely took more abuse than we ever deserved—assuming we ever deserved any of it. If we have reached this point, we can trust that we were pushed to it by our toxic family members. We must never feel guilty for protecting ourselves with the no-contact option.

Keep in mind, our toxic family members feel no guilt and have never been sorry for harming us. We have every right to protect ourselves from those who manipulate and emotionally abuse us. At one point we loved our toxic family members and wanted them in our lives more than anything else. Yet at too many points in time, we sacrificed our happiness to serve theirs, shut our mouth when we desperately wanted to speak up, and did what they wanted because doing that was easier than dealing with their drama. We must understand that our toxic family members have simply walked us to the door we're now choosing to shut.

Healing Moment

 If it's hurting you more than it's healing you, love yourself enough to let it go.

Important Questions to Ask before Going No Contact

- Does this person ever admit wrong?
- Does this person ever genuinely apologize and change his or her behavior?
- Does this person show remorse for what he or she has done?
- Has this person ever validated your perception as right?
- Does this person respect the limits or boundaries that you've set?
- Is this person willing to do anything and everything to make a relationship with you work?

If the answers to these questions are undoubtedly no, then you need to consider cutting ties.

This decision is more forced upon us than it is voluntary, and it's confusing because we're conditioned to believe that terminating relationships with family is morally wrong. However, our toxic family members are just people and not always healthy people. In reality, if these individuals were not our family members, we would never choose them to be part of our lives. Under the ideal of family, we spend years sacrificing our mental and emotional health under the notion that we *have to* make this sacrifice because these people are family. We are conditioned to believe that if we end relationships with them, we are bad people. No one wants to feel that they are inherently bad.

Nevertheless, here is what I know for sure. It is far better to make the decision to go no contact and break our own heart than it is to stay in a relationship in which our toxic family members break our heart over and over.

In an article I wrote for the *Huffington Post* in 2016, I discussed the hard truth about when and why we may need to cut ties with our toxic family members in order to save ourselves. You need to go no contact …

- When the relationship is based in any type of abuse mentally, physically, sexually, verbally, or emotionally.
- When the only contact you have with them is negative.
- When the relationship creates so much stress that it impacts the important areas of your life at work or home.
- When you find yourself obsessed with the gossip about you and trying to right wrong information and constantly being ostracized to the point you are losing sleep over it.
- When the relationship is all about the other person and there is no real reason why the other person cannot make any effort toward the health and maintenance of the relationship with you.
- When crazy-making, no-win games dominate the relationship—such as the silent treatment, blame-games, and no-win arguments that spin around on you.

As these characteristics mount up in a given relationship, you need to pay them heed and consider breaking away from the relationship.

Before you choose to go no contact, I highly recommend that you have a loving support system in place to reassure yourself that you will not be alone once you make this change. What you have to be prepared for is the response of your toxic family members. They will likely do all they can to isolate you by targeting your key supports to do what they can to turn them against you. Once you see the smear campaign is in full effect, you must come to trust that you need to stay quiet and not engage. Just let it happen and let it pass. The more you fight the smearing, the bigger the gossip and lies become and the crazier you will look to others. Our toxic family members smear us for the sole purpose of trying to rob us of the very support system we need and deserve to have in place. They want to ensure we are robbed of having a soft place to fall and that we do not have people on our side supporting our decision. I have witnessed my mother do this time and again. Luckily, I live in a different state, and the people closest to me now are not persons she has any influence over.

Our toxic family members want us to have nowhere to go but back to them. The intention behind this is deeply hurtful and somewhat terrifying, for our family members may use this opportunity to do as much harm to us as they can. Note, however, that they do not want us letting their secrets into the light, and they absolutely do not want to lose the power they have had in controlling and dominating our lives.

To us, their type of behavior is unthinkable. It is deeply cruel and manipulative. But what we have to keep in mind is that only insecure, toxic people would ever respond in this way. This reaction, although hurtful and scary to us, is second nature to poisonous individuals. They do not have it in them to keep love in their lives in healthy ways because they are not healthy.

If *we* want to be healthy, we must prepare for the time that when we leave our toxic family members, we will likely also be forced to leave behind many others who connect us to them. We must be okay with this, embracing it as an acceptable loss. I have experienced in my own life and watched others who have also been in a similar position have things turn out better than fine when they make these decisions. In some ways this is a blind journey, to be sure. We cannot predict all that will happen. But I believe whenever we activate positively for our mental and emotional health, we find that what has been left gaping and empty in our lives will eventually be replaced by situations and people that are better and healthier for us.

Why No Contact Hurts and Why It Works

No contact is never the choice any of us want to make. But no contact is the only healthy choice our toxic family members leave us with.

I have experienced my own going no contact as similar to a death; the only difference is that my toxic family members are still alive walking upon this earth. I know that in the event that any one of my toxic family members passes away,

I am blessed with the certainty that their death and absence from my life while they were alive were no fault of my own.

Getting to this point has not been easy. Hypothetically, had any one of them died, because I have worked so hard through the no-contact option, I would have been free from grave self-doubts. I would not have had to wrestle with deep self-questioning over my personal rights to take care of myself and have my own opinions, my lovability as a human being, or my not being at fault for their anger, unhappiness, and rejection of me. I have settled these issues for myself. This process, however, has been challenging and painful. My toxic family members refuse to own what they've done to force this separation. Each day they choose to lay the fault solely upon me is another day they emotionally abandon me, invalidate my experience, and scapegoat me with the blame. They completely disregard how all of this has impacted me over the course of my life. I have had to work hard in my own therapy to not question myself and to reject laying the fault of the demise of our relationship solely upon myself.

Going no contact hurts, and yet, it is the one thing that gives me the space and time I need to heal and find my own sense of life and happiness. I can say that the further away I get from my family members' abusive patterns, the more I realize how deeply and consistently I was always and in all ways manipulated. Gaining this understanding has been liberating and helpful to the strength I need to carry on alone in my life. I have come to understand that at first, we go no contact because we absolutely feel that we *have* to, but after some time of being in that no-contact condition, we find that we remain in it because we *want* to.

Healing Moment

 No contact is not put in place to hurt anyone. Rather, it is done to protect us.

As we stay in no contact, our toxic family members will eventually quiet down, and there will be fewer people who care about their smearing and the victimized story they tell of our cruelty. As things settle, our anxiety decreases, and we begin to experience peace and freedom in ways we have never experienced before. The further away we get from our toxic family members, the more we can't imagine ever going back to that level of drama and dysfunction in our lives. Time away and personal space help us gain perspective. We may also begin to feel deeply thankful we were able to find the strength and self-love to stop their chaos in our lives.

Ignore to Hurt vs. No Contact to Protect

I have had many moments of questioning myself around no contact because I never want to be like my toxic family members. I've sat with many patients who experience the same confusion over this option that I have had.

What is the difference between the silent treatment" abusers use and going no contact, which we can use to set protective boundaries for ourselves? We may wonder, *How am I any different from my toxic family members if I cut ties and go silent?* The difference comes down to intent.

When our toxic family members ghost us or give us the silent treatment, their intent is to make us feel ostracized, left out, hurt, insecure, and abandoned. They want to put us into a state of fear and panic so we will plead to be a part of their lives again. They toy with our sense of security to get this result. Yet, we've all been through the discarding phase of their abuse and know that the more we beg, try to be good, and work to convince or please our toxic family members, the further away they retract, which only deepens our feelings of rejection. This keeps us chasing them. When this manipulation is going on, it seems as if the only thing we can focus on is why we are being shut out. It pulls us away from all the good in our life. We forget we have the power to leave our situation. This is exactly what our toxic family members want.

However, when we decide to go no contact as a healthy and necessary form of setting boundaries, our intent is not to hurt anyone else. We choose to go silent with the intention to protect ourselves. Moreover, we go silent and stay silent. We have no want, need, or desire to hurt the toxic family members in our lives by toying with them in any way. We go no contact to remove their abuse from our life permanently. When we cut ties, the relationship is severed. We let it go. Our intent is not to look back but to move forward. When we go no contact, we have no other agenda than protecting our emotional well-being. Further, our decision is based in knowing we did all we could to forgive our toxic family and give them chance after chance to change.

Healing Moment

If we go no contact, we have reached the place where enough is enough.

Abandonment vs. No Contact

Another important difference is between no contact and abandonment. Without understanding it, you can fall down a rabbit hole of self-doubt and guilt.

We don't want to feel as if we have harshly and hurtfully abandoned our toxic family members. That's a horrible feeling—one that any healthy person would seek to avoid at all cost. What we need to remember, though, is we can only abandon someone we love and who we know wants and will do anything to be a significant part of our life. No contact is something we are forced to choose whenever we're in a position to protect ourselves. We cease contact because, if we don't, we open our lives to our toxic family members and their continual lies, manipulations, blame, control, trickery, guilt, humiliation, intimidation, guilt, projection, false hope, and abandonment.

One thing I learned in my own personal therapy is that all relationships, whether we've gone no contact or someone has passed away, still have an ongoing side to them. Instead of viewing our decision to go no contact as cutting our toxic family members off in the sense of our ignoring them or abandoning them, we can look at it from the vantage point that we have simply changed the *form* of the relationship we share with them. The relationship used to be active and verbal, and now it is quiet and non-verbal. We will still think about our toxic family members, but we will have a distant and silent relationship with them that is void of their abuse and manipulation. The relationship is now silent and ordered rather than dramatic and chaotic.

Healing Moment

The relationship is still there. It is just silent.

I choose to look at the silent relationships I have with my toxic family members this way: the relationships are irreparably injured and now paralyzed. Just because a person loses the function of their legs when physically paralyzed doesn't mean their brain stops sending signals to their legs. The brain still sends out consistent signals (thoughts) to their legs as if their legs are still working. The signal simply can't get past where the injury occurred in the spinal cord. We can use this metaphor for our silent relationships with our toxic family members. Our family members are still there, but our relationship with them simply doesn't work anymore. The thoughts and emotions we send out about our toxic family members can't get past the emotional injuries to our heart.

It also takes time to adjust and adapt to our new life, just like it does for a paraplegic. In fact, it's a lifetime of adjustment. Setting no-contact boundaries doesn't mean we stop loving our family members or that we don't still long for them, just as a paraplegic still yearns for the use of his legs. Setting no-contact limits means that having our toxic family members as functional and useful parts of our lives just isn't an option anymore. We will never regain our "use" of them; therefore, we will have to grieve that loss and adapt to life without them.

Setting Limits Guilt-Free

Think about what it means to set healthy and appropriate limits on our children. When we set limits on their behavior, enforce consequences, refuse to condone certain behaviors of theirs, and do all we can to teach them right from wrong by making it clear which behaviors we expect from them, we are considered good and loving parents. We are viewed as parents who love their children enough to teach them right from wrong, to be kind, honest, and respectful toward others, to live their lives with a sense of grace, and possess a conscience. The best way to teach our children these important values is to live these values fully in our own lives. This type of parenting and role modeling is reflective of the depth of love we have for our children, that we show concern for how they show up in life.

I question why operating in this way and having these same expectations are treated completely differently when we apply these to the ways our toxic family members treat us. It seems logical to me that we should expect our family members to treat us with compassion, respect, honesty, kindness, and a sense of forethought in how something they may or may not do could be hurtful to us. It makes sense to me that it is appropriate to set limits on the behaviors our toxic family members use that cause us great pain. Why is it, then, that when we set limits on our children's poor behavior, we're considered great parents, but when we set these same limits on the hurtful behaviors of our toxic family members, we are considered heartless and cruel? How does this make sense? Aren't we setting limits on our toxic family members with the same type of love and compassion we use to appropriately parent our children? Isn't this type of behavior also an indication that we love our toxic family members enough to want to give them an opportunity to understand and change their abusive ways?

Setting limits on abusers is not unloving, including when we do this with our toxic family members. In fact, the reason we try so hard for so long to work things out with our toxic family *is* precisely because we love them!

Not everyone understands this. Some people outside of our abusers will judge our choices as cold, cruel, and uncaring. I believe we should exercise some compassion toward our critics. They are unaware and unfamiliar with what emotional abuse and manipulation look like and how deeply they impact our self-worth and fulfillment in life. We have to come to a place within our own self where flourishing in our life supersedes the opinions and lack of understanding other people have of our situation.

Healing Moment

 A harsh fact of life is that there are some people we can hold in our heart but cannot have in our life.

Questions and Answers

Taking the no-contact option involves more than us. If we have children of our own, our decision impacts them. And then there will be others in our circle of friends and work associates who may wonder why we chose to separate from certain family members. Here I want to address some questions the no-contact decision raises.

What do we tell our children about no contact?

A parent's number one duty in life is to protect his or her children. When it comes to telling our children about no contact with their grandparents, we must keep a few things in mind.

Danu Morrigan makes it clear that "we have every right and indeed the responsibility to protect our children from abusers no matter who they are."[21] Our society seems to view mothers and grandparents to be of higher status than other family members, but if our parents (our children's grandparents) are emotionally abusive, we still must hold firm to protecting our children from them. When we protect our children from abusers, whether the abusers are family members or not, we are not taking anything healthy away from them. We are saving our children from emotional pain, triangulation, manipulation, fakeness, hurt, and confusion.

Our children aren't nearly as conditioned by life and people as we are. Yet they always seem to know more than we give them credit for. So it is important to be honest and vulnerable with our children by providing them with the obvious and clear reasons the relationships with our toxic family members dissolved and how this dissolution will impact their life. The last thing our children want is to see us constantly hurting. In protecting ourselves, we also protect them. When we set no-contact boundaries with those who persistently damage us, we model to our children the importance of boundaries and what it looks like to maintain self-respect. We teach our children that not all relationships can be worked out between all people. These are some of life's more challenging facts our children deserve to learn as early as possible. We are teaching them that just because some people are family does not mean they are loving, caring individuals and should get away with their abuse because of this title.

Healing Moment

The most important thing for our children to see and admire in us is our ability to love ourselves enough to make the proper relationship decisions that free us to live and function as optimally as we can.

What do we tell other people about no contact?

People who do not understand that toxic individuals can include mothers, fathers, children, grandparents, and the like will erroneously judge us in a negative light. They may not think we're bad persons, but they hold a belief that all things between people can eventually work out. What they don't realize is that this is only true among healthy people. Toxic people use our forgiveness to further manipulate and abuse us. Once we forgive, they get the message they can push their manipulating even further the next time. But there is no need to further our hurt. Nor do we owe any person who hasn't walked a mile in our shoes an explanation for the relationship decisions we've been forced to make. Life is not life at all if we have to justify insanity to stay in relationships. However, we will be asked and people will be curious as to why we have no contact with our family members.

Here's what we can tell people: "My family members suffer from an incurable and progressive personality disorder that prevents them from treating me with love, respect, or kindness. Because they have this personality disorder, it means they cannot and will not look at how they hurt me or others, which gives them no chance at change or getting better. This is why it is best for me to keep distance between myself and them." When we can explain and justify our experience of the toxic people in our lives in clinical terms, it puts our listeners into a mind-set of learning rather than judging. I have found I am taken more seriously when I explain that my toxic family members have an incurable form of emotional cancer. This isn't a condition they caught, and they have no excuse or justification for it. I find that I receive fewer questions and less doubt when I communicate this way. It also protects me from my listeners saying, "But it's your family."

Can we cut ties with our own children?

It is our job as parents to teach our children right from wrong. If they are treating us disrespectfully, using or abusing us in any way, whether that be financial, verbal, physical, or emotional, cutting ties may be our only choice to teach them right from wrong. There isn't a parent out there who wants to face this decision. There is perhaps no greater pain because no matter how horrible our children may be behaving, we love them.

I treat a couple whose youngest son has always been quick to anger. He has rejected any and all efforts they have made toward disciplining him and helping him in other ways. He doesn't make enough money to move out on his own, and he is emotionally and physically violent in the home. His parents have taken him to psychiatrists, life coaches, and psychologists for help. I told the parents I would not treat their son but I would treat them. I read to them some of H. G. Tudor's book *Manipulated* in session, and we knew we had found the problem. Their son thrives off of emotional reaction and attention, and this is the one thing they needed to take away from their son if he had any chance of making healthy changes. At the beginning of treatment, these parents had to learn to harness their reactions to him. The less they reacted to their son, the more he upped the ante. I encouraged these parents to continue to not react. They followed my lead, and soon their son's behavior began changing for the better. It took time, trust, and education in the world of narcissistic manipulation for them to start finding a balance. It also took an incredibly painful toll on them emotionally, but these parents understood that the worst mistake they could make with their son was to let him keep manipulating and abusing them.

As they moved into a nonreactive parenting style, at first they felt as if they weren't disciplining their son at all, that they were allowing him to get away with the unbelievable. They found this approach frustrating and painful. I explained to them that we cannot parent toxic people with the parenting skills we would use with healthy children. When someone is toxic, we have to apply an inverse technique to parenting, which involves not rewarding bad behavior with any attention or emotional reaction. In the case that our children don't respond to any form of discipline, like the thirty-year-old male in the news whose parents had to take him to court to evict him from their home,[22] then we have to make decisions to cut ties no matter how painful that may be.

Death and No Contact

What happens if or when our toxic family members die? Will we feel guilty about going no contact?

One day our toxic family members will pass away. This matter about death almost always comes up whenever we consider the option of initiating no-contact boundaries. It pulls on our empathy, our morality, and on the needs we have to feel safe and happy.

This issue popped up for me many times right after I initiated no contact. I constantly questioned myself:

- Will I feel like a bad daughter or sister for staying away from them for all these years and now one of them has died?
- Is it really too late to make things better?
- Can I live with myself if one of my toxic family members dies?
- Will I feel guilty?
- Will I feel bad about myself?
- Will I punish myself for the rest of my life?
- What will other people think?

The answer to these questions will be unique from individual to individual.

If you think you could never live with yourself should a family member die, then this is a valid reason to continue having some level of contact with your toxic family members. However, I must warn you that there is a price to pay for this choice—it puts you in the position to be continually manipulated. If the death questions and the guilt or doubt that may come along with them are just too painful to face, you have to change your perception on staying in contact with your toxic family. You must consciously view your choice to stay in contact as something you are doing for *you* and for your own emotional health rather than as anything you are doing to benefit them. But I challenge you to consider the fact that your toxic family members will pass away as all living things do, so isn't staying in contact just a get-out-of-jail-free card that you use as an excuse that allows you to be continually abused so you can avoid some type of guilt?

And guilt for what?

How can we justify our own unnatural and intentional emotional rape or homicide as a less important death than the natural death of our toxic family members? They don't intend to die, but they did repeatedly choose to emotionally abuse us.

I think we each deserve better.

Danu Morrigan has concluded that any guilt we would feel after one of our toxic family members died would be a false guilt. We can only be guilty if we have done something wrong, spiteful, or cruel to another person. Protecting ourselves by going no contact with the toxic family members who have psychologically abused us is not wrong. Morrigan encourages us to look at our choice in the deathbed call from the much more accurate perspective that our toxic family members have had years upon years to genuinely work things out with us, but they have ignored or not taken advantage of any of those opportunities. Therefore, guilt of any kind should not be laid upon us but upon them. She further explains that a deathbed meeting ultimately cannot end well because it is unlikely that our toxic family members will use their dying as an opportunity to take accountability for how they have treated us. They have had a plethora of time to give us the validation and apologies we have been looking for and deserved, even though they may have sent random cards or gifts for the holidays over the years as a way to make themselves look good and portray us as stubborn grudge-holders. What they have never done is ask, "What's wrong, and how can we fix the problems between us?"

Morrigan contends that if we were to accept a fake apology at a deathbed moment, we would essentially be helping our toxic family members in our own abuse. We would be assisting them in invalidating the experience we've had with them over the duration of our life, thereby deleting any of their accountability for all of the hurt, pain, and abandonment they've inflicted upon us. Such an act on our part is equivalent to our engaging in our own self-abandonment.

We must love ourselves more than this. The laws of cause and effect are what they are for a reason. It is important for us to remain in a place of protecting ourselves and valuing our worth, even when that means our toxic family members lose their relationship with us, and this, unfortunately, includes the moments they are on their deathbed. Their loss of a relationship with us is the naturally occurring consequence to come from a lifetime of their abuse and manipulation.

Healing Moment

Setting limits on our toxic family members has not a thing to do with a lack of love or holding grudges; it has everything to do with personal safety. We can set boundaries and limits on people and still love them.

No Contact—A Personal View

I love my family. I also don't like them.

I no longer make the choice to host people in my life that I do not or cannot like. If I dislike someone, it is not because I am heartless. There is a good reason for my feeling this way. The most loving thing I can do for myself is set the necessary boundaries that hold me tight and keep me safe from people who intentionally seek to bring me down. In doing this, I give myself the opportunity to live a life I love rather than living a life I fear and dread. I do not believe there is anything wrong with expecting people to treat me with decency.

When I cut my final ties to my toxic family members and the extraneous people who connected me to them, I felt afraid at first. I felt like I was doomed to be alone the rest of my life without any kind of support. But the emotional chaos and abuse of being connected to them just wasn't worth the self-sacrifice anymore.

Once I let go of them and took the necessary steps to build a protective fortress around myself and my daughter, I truly felt like I had finally been released from thick, invisible, psychological tethers that had been holding me to a solid, huge, heavy, black metal ball of emotional pain and obligation. I was no longer in prison. I was free!

At the same time, I felt a deep aloneness. My newfound freedom was unfamiliar. The only life I had known was one in which I was tied to and within that bleak, despairing darkness of family abuse. That black heavy ball of stress made me feel as if I belonged somewhere, even if it was only to the familiar feelings of sadness, pain, fury, and confusion. That ball of stress was what I knew as home, and I have *some* good memories of that time that were not painful. But when I look at the percentages, I can see that I was miserable and emotionally suffering 95 percent of the time. And I really am unsure if the 5 percent joy I felt growing up was ever real or if it was just the counterfeit kindness my toxic family members knew I needed as a way to keep me from leaving my position as the family scapegoat.

It took awhile, but I finally accepted the fact that it just wasn't worth it for me to stay connected to my toxic family. Is 5 percent or less of happiness worth all the drama, manipulation, hurt, and damage they caused? And even that is tainted with the likelihood that those happy times were faked and plagued with deceptive forms of manipulation. I at last untethered myself from them completely. I finally accepted that my toxic family members were never going to love and support me in the ways I needed and deserved. I was tired of exhausting myself to be "lovable" in their eyes.

Not needing their approval set me strongly into the development of my own sense of self, my own purpose in life, and much healthier relationships. The decision took forty-two years with my father and brother and until I was forty-five with my mother. I can say when I made these difficult and painful decisions, I was as certain as I could be under circumstances such as these that I was doing the right thing because I had tried everything else.

Today I feel more strongly than ever that I made the best decision. I still feel loss, but I am finally done with all the anxiety, rejection, confusion, neediness, and pleasing I did to fit in with my toxic family.

The loss is something I can deal with.

What I cannot deal with is their continued abuse. I finally put an end to that.

Healing Moment

 I do not hate my toxic family members. I also do not need them.

I feel mostly free and happy without my toxic family members in my life. Sometimes I am also still sad. I am sad that they are who they are toward me as they all seem to fit just fine with each other. I know I am not like them, even though I always wanted to be when I was growing up and didn't understand my circumstances. I am also content to say that my sadness dulls over time as a deeper sense of acceptance sinks into my heart. I can also accept that my circumstances are sad and unfortunate. I will always grieve my fantasy family. I will always grieve a bit over what I feel I deserved to have in terms of family. Yet, as I continue to grow in and experience my life, I understand and accept a hard truth about things—about people. People can be inherently self-seeking. I know firsthand that not all people have good intentions, even when we are related to them, even when they are our parents or other family members. I have come to see that my toxic family members are just people. They are not powers. If I were not related to them by blood, I would never choose any of them for friends, and they would not choose me. In fact, they have never chosen me. They are just people, and they are not my people.

It is my job to fill my life with *my* people—the ones who love me without condition, the ones who love me for me, the ones who uplift me, who could never fathom hurting me intentionally, the ones who are proud of me, who hold me tight when I am in pain, and who support my drive to feel happy, fulfilled, and successful. My people include those who have witnessed the manipulation I've had to bear and who have seen how hard I have tried and how many times I have forgiven my toxic family members, only to have them repeat their abusive patterns with me. My people are those who love me for having the courage to leave behind the pain consistently inflicted upon me. They include the new people who have come into my life and the few who have always been there to kiss and love me back to life. I have learned from these people that blood is not thicker than love. Love is thicker than blood.

Healing Moment

Our toxic family members are foolish to believe we won't get to a point where we will tire of the ridiculous ways in which they manipulate us and finally put a stop to it.

Lyric Therapy

So I cut you off
I don't need your love
'Cause I already cried enough
I've been movin' on since we said goodbye
—"Dua Lipa," by IDGAF[23]

9

Hoovering: Separation Abuse

The term *hoovering* is named after the Hoover vacuum cleaner. It is used to refer to a form of abuse—specifically, separation abuse. Hoovering is a technique toxic people use in an effort to "suck" their victims back into a relationship with them. It is a premeditated appeal to our good nature.

Hoovering occurs most often in the first year after we establish no contact with our toxic family members. And it comes during those times when it would be easiest to catch us at a weak moment—a moment in which we may feel susceptible, sentimental, or nostalgic. Our toxic family members hoover to manipulate and toy with our emotions to provoke a reaction from us. If we give any reaction, whether positive or negative, our toxic family members will interpret it to mean that we still care, and if we still care, then there's still hope. Hope for what? The hope to be able to continue to own manipulative control over us. Our toxic family members do not want us to move on in our lives, to be independent from them. So whether they've disowned us or we establish a wall of silence between us and them, we cannot count on them staying away from us.

For our toxic family members, a separation is treated as a competition. If we go no contact, some of our toxic family members will ignore us to give us a taste of our own medicine. Or, they will go silent as a way to make us feel we never mattered to them in the first place.

Others will hoover by inserting themselves into the critical relationships in our lives and try to create destruction to threaten and scare us. For example, the ex-wife of a patient of mine was messaging and calling his new girlfriend, telling her that he was a pathological narcissist and psychopath. She used overly dramatic language and was begging his new girlfriend to call her so they could talk and she could save his new girlfriend's life from his wrath. This same ex-wife also wrote a letter to all of my patient's family members pleading for money to pay for one of their sons to go to a private school, claiming my patient refused to pay. My patient actually didn't believe their son needed private school, and he was already paying his ex upwards of one hundred thousand dollars per year in support. His family, feeling afraid of the ex-wife not letting them see his children if they didn't pay the money, gave it to his ex-wife for my patient's son's private school. This woman lies about her finances, including telling their children that my patient steals money from her. She has spent up to sixty thousand dollars on her attorney, even though she only gets three years of support. She's an emotional nightmare and manipulator. She creates compliance through the use of manipulating other people with their own fears. She doesn't move on, find a new life, or do anything differently to support herself. Instead, she hoovers. She sucks at the old life she shared with him—the one she single-handedly destroyed herself.

Some other toxic family members will take to social media and try to make us feel left out and hurt through this outlet. This means we must block all of our social media accounts to protect ourselves from seeing what they are doing or venting about when it comes to us. Whatever we see from them on social media, it's most likely designed to provoke us and harm us.

Still other toxic family members will beg, plead, stalk, and act completely victimized, leaving us confused over why they're so hurt when they were so cruel toward us.

If we fall for any of their hoovering, they will suck us back in for the sole purpose of exacting revenge once they feel confident they have secured our trust. They will never let us live down setting healthy boundaries and leaving them behind. But the worst thing we can put ourselves through is going back to those individuals who lived to hurt us. Each time we go back, we take an even bigger drop in our self-worth. Each time we go back, it's harder to leave. We have to remain aware of who we're really dealing with—toxic family members who don't have the capacity for genuine attachments. They can only *act* as if they care.

Once we're out of these poisonous relationships, recovery is extremely hard. We didn't just lose who we thought our family members were. We also lost who we thought *we* were. We lost trust in ourselves to make healthy decisions. So we must remember that if we give an inch, our toxic family members will take ten miles.

Healing Moment

We must stand guard to protect our sensitivities and good nature.

Hoovering Tactics

Toxic family members often engage in hoovering after they have received the silent treatment from their victim or been left behind. Hoovering often starts off subtle and innocent and is done through voicemail, text messages, dropping things off, needing to pick things up, email, phone calls, notes, other people, or through any other form of possible communication with the victim. Because toxic people know our weak spots, they tend to target these areas in order to re-establish communication. Once communication is reopened, toxic people make grandiose promises of change and tell us exactly what our broken hearts want to hear. The changes they profess to make never happen for any length of time, and we end up feeling like the Peanuts cartoon characters, Charlie Brown and Lucy. Each time Lucy holds the football for Charlie Brown and he goes to kick to the ball, she pulls it away and enjoys watching him fall.

Here are some clear examples of hoovering.

- *Brainwashing others into believing we are crazy and they are innocent.* After I chose to stop mending fences with my mother, she immediately went for the people I care about most and told them I was a monster and that "she doesn't know what gets into me." She lies about my mental health as a way to jump in front of the truth and destroy my credibility. To this day she runs around our small town advertising and martyring to anyone who will listen that I don't talk to her. And people believe what she tells them.

- *Stalking us, driving by our house, and taking photos of us without our consent.* I had an ex-boyfriend who passively stalked me for over a year. I would see his car four different times on a five-mile run; he would drop things off "for me" at the leasing office of my housing complex; he would create new email addresses to get around my online blocks so he could ask me if I had seen some random item while I was packing. Other toxic people will hire private investigators or put our phones on location and question us about where we are and what we're doing. The large majority of people will stalk our social media and accuse us online and offline of being bad people.

- *Threatening that bad things might happen to us.* It is common to receive threats of suicide if we don't do what the toxic person wants us to do. This is their way of manipulating our fears so deeply that we will come back into their lives.

- *Leaving unwanted gifts for us or performing favors without our permission.* Many toxic people use gift-giving as a way to manipulate. My mother sends Christmas gifts and birthday cards that are "sickie sweet," as if nothing has ever gone wrong between us.

- *Entering our house while we're out.* Toxic people can feel so entitled that they will do whatever it takes, no matter how invasive, to show us they can and will do whatever they want, including entering our house when we're not home. I had one patient whose father unexpectedly showed up at his son's house on his birthday and refused to leave. The police had to be called to escort this man off his son's property.

- *Colluding with our ex-spouse, children, friends, or therapist.* My mother immediately connected with my ex-husband after not speaking to him for ten years to triangulate and involve him in her manipulation.
- *Giving us gifts on "duty days" (holidays, birthdays, illnesses, deaths, anniversaries, births).* Toxic people want to appear as if they are good-hearted. They use holidays, known as "holiday hoovering," as the perfect opportunity to make themselves appear like the bigger person, the hurt and abandoned person, who is making efforts to mend fences. In reality, the gifts have nothing to do with us, and they certainly do not intend to convey any authentic sense of remorse or ownership on the part of the toxic giver. Instead, toxic persons use these gifts so they look like the "good" ones. This activity allows them to say to others, "I've tried. I have sent presents and cards, but she's so mean and stubborn that she just holds a grudge."
- *Enlisting other family members or close friends to spy on us, relay messages to us, or gather information on us and what we're doing.* Many toxic people use social media as an outlet to spy on us. Although my mother isn't on social media, many people whom she is close to are, and I am quite aware of who her lieutenants are online. I have blocked most everyone who is connected to her on a family level and had to set boundaries on my mom's sister around bringing my mother up to me in private messages and taking any opportunity she could to bring her up publicly on my Facebook page. Thankfully, my aunt has been respectful of the boundaries I've set.
- *Circumventing us by going behind our back to contact our spouse or children in an attempt to maintain a relationship with them that doesn't include us.* Many toxic parents do all they can to work around the boundaries we've set on them by triangulating those who are closest to us. They do this as a way to demonstrate they are above boundaries and refuse to take no for an answer. They are going to do what they want and how they want regardless of how hurtful or damaging it is to us and all others involved. They view anyone who is connected to us, and this includes our children, as weapons for warfare.

- *Sending us memorabilia from our childhood to pull on our heartstrings.* One year my mother sent me a bronze of a mother swinging a daughter. Interestingly enough, the bronze arrived broken at the base. It also wasn't packed in a box labeled as fragile—a step my mother always took in the past. If you know anything about a bronze, they are near to impossible to break. I believe it was sent broken to be a cryptic symbol, and every other gift I received that Christmas had something to do with mothering or being a mom. The entire effort made me sick.
- *Sending gifts that are all about "family."* Many disgruntled ex-spouses will send us pictures of who and how we were as a family to show us what we have allegedly ruined.

The Intention behind Hoovering

The separation abuse behind hoovering is meant to provoke in us feelings of guilt and obligation and to send us the following messages:

- "Remember all the good times we had? Don't you miss them?"
- "Can't you see that I am normal and nice? Look at all that I have done for you!"
- "We are family. You owe me a relationship with you."
- "Here's proof that I do care about your feelings."
- "If you think I am going to let you say no to me, you're wrong."
- "Why should I let you go and have a nice life without including me in it?"
- "I will stir the pot whether you like it or not. I am entitled to you."
- "I will make you think about me."
- "I will provoke a reaction from you for my enjoyment."
- "I will force you to pay attention to me."
- "I will not let you do well without me."

When I look at the hoovering I've undergone in my own family dynamics, I can see how members either bullied me back into the relationship with overt or covert threats or lies or showed up only on "duty days."

Two years ago, I put my relationship with my mother into an active state of silence. Since that time, she has sent me and my daughter duty-day presents or cards on designated holidays, namely Christmas and birthdays. She doesn't reach out or make efforts outside of those days. In my first year of silence with her, I found it quite ironic that she sent Christmas and birthday presents but nothing for Mother's Day. That passive-aggressive move helped me see that her presents were simply fraudulent. The bottom line is I am still her daughter all the other days of the year too. But if she chose to give me presents on any of the other days, especially the ones that aren't holidays, she wouldn't look as good to others, or so she thinks, and my sensitivities would be far less vulnerable to her manipulations. So her gift-giving is severely restricted; there's no reason for her to bother on any of the other days. Instead she uses the other 363 days of the year to lament on and on about how I've cut her off while she has even sent me gifts and cards trying to mend our relationship. Of course, she has a host of other ways to get in touch with me if that was what she really wanted. And she has no problem getting her cards and presents to my house. Yet, she complains to my ex-husband that I keep my daughter from her, that she never gets to see her or hear from her. What my mother has proved to me is that she is a master at making herself out to be the victim, regardless of the circumstances and the truth of the situation.

I find her duty-day presents to be the most interesting, fake, and offensive. Her cards say loving words, but they are just words. She acts as if nothing has ever happened between us. These duty-day gifts are meant to maintain her own public image of being a good mother, but they only serve to falsify the veracity of her mothering. The public image of her is drastically different than the reality of the daily abandonment and vile rejection she carries out in our relationship in private. Her cards will say that she loves me always and holds me close to her heart and that any time *I* am ready to come back, *her* arms are wide open. Apparently, she holds me close to her heart one to two times per year, for that's how often the cards come. In reality, she sends presents and writes these false words because it makes her feel good about herself and gives her ammunition to tell others how much she tries to reach out to me even though I am so mean to her. The subtext behind her false-love words is clear: *I* am at fault, *I* need to get over it, and *I* am hurting *her*.

Every time my mother sends passive-aggressive gifts and cards my way, she is a perpetrator.

Every time she calls my ex-husband to get him to side with her, she's a perpetrator.

Every time she trashes me to our close family friends and others I know, she is a perpetrator.

The truth about who she is and what she's about is clear to me. I will not be subject to her anymore.

Healing Moment

Showing up on duty days is not a sign that our toxic family members are being nice to us; instead it indicates that they are trying to guilt us and manipulate us.

My mother's duty-day gifts are meant to be intrusive and controlling, not loving and mending. If she sends gifts, I am forced to think about her and deal with her on some level when it's the last thing I want to do. Our toxic family members force themselves into these days as a way to bully us. We may have moved on from them to the best of our ability, but they haven't moved on from us. They are always plotting and conniving to find ways, any way, they can to get us to respond to them.

No one has the right to tell us we cannot be left alone if that's what we need and want for ourselves. Anyone who invasively crosses that limit over and over again is a person who has no respect for what we need, desire, or want. It can be easy to confuse invasiveness with love and interest, which is why many of us break down on meeting our own needs to give our toxic family members the attention they want. But all we are doing is temporarily avoiding conflict. And the more we do this, the more we lose touch with what our personal rights are.

Make no mistake that our toxic family members view our patience with their offensive behavior as a vulnerability for them to exploit. Our love and passivity toward them are how they have gotten away with abusing us. We learn the hard way that no matter how much we love them, serve them, try our hardest for them, change ourselves, succeed, and so on, what we do will never be enough. They will not love us in return. They view our efforts toward pleasing them with a sense of contempt because they're consumed with jealousy and envy. They don't want to see us doing well or being good people. It is the good that we naturally hold within us they seek to kill.

Healing Moment

A toxic person will always have someone to accuse of ruining their life. It is invariably the same person the toxic person is trying to destroy.

Caring about What Other People Think?

One of the main reasons that I and many others have done all we can to avoid establishing no contact is because we would rather be chronically abused than face the smear campaign and hoovering that occurs once we cut ties. Toxic people target those we love the most. Because we are human, we naturally care about what other people think of us. The thought of everyone being turned against us and imagining being all alone keeps us too afraid to leave our toxic family in an effort to keep the other people we love in our lives. We end up feeling like we have to choose the lesser of two evils. Our toxic family members will have no qualms over assassinating our character. They will use the hoovering method to exact revenge and provoke a response from us. Hoovering will be a means to influence others we care about to develop an extremely negative perception of us. Our toxic family members will manipulate facts, slander us, start rumors, and contact all of the people we value in order to paint an untrue picture of us. This sets us up to receive unfair, unwarranted, and excessive criticism and false judgments that we will have to spend countless hours trying to undo.

The smear campaign is often the most feared consequence because we are human and we genuinely care about what other people think. As healthy people, we hate it if there is an untruth being spread about us, and we will have the impulse to go to everyone who has been told the lies to explain what the truth really is. Unfortunately, with a smear campaign, by the time we reach the people who have been led astray, the damage has already been done.

The staggering thing about this tactic, at least from my experience, is that people who have known us for many years can actually be duped by the lies.

They can find our toxic family members so believable that they forget what they know to be true about us in favor of the lies they have been told. I find this utterly heartbreaking. They could simply say to our toxic family members, "We love Sherrie, and we love you, so whatever issues you have with her cannot be discussed with us." This, however, rarely happens. Our toxic family members are great manipulators. They prey upon people who have good hearts and who believe all parents love their children and that all siblings get along. Tragically, such people too often assume that our toxic family members must be telling them the truth about us. I have had to conclude that if we have to spend hours trying to convince people who know us deeply that we are not the bad ones, they are not truly our people. If I have to defend myself to a person who knows me well, that person becomes someone I can no longer trust with my heart.

In spite of the damage our toxic family members can do even when we choose the no-contact path, I still believe going no contact is worth it. When we establish no contact, we receive the gift of discovering the truth about others. We get to discover who genuinely loves us as opposed to those who may have just been a decoration but not a genuine support. I look at the smear campaign as the greatest way for us to weed out the true loves from the false or weak loves in our lives. And that turns out to be one of the best gifts we can ever give ourselves.

Healing Moment

 It is natural to care about what other people think, but we don't have to give any power to this when it comes to making decisions around our emotional and mental well-being.

Lyric Therapy
I can't keep up with your turning tables
Under your thumb, I can't breathe
So I won't let you close enough to hurt me
—"Turning Tables," by Adele[24]

10

What about God?

R egardless of what type of family we come from, we are told by religious texts, ideals from the world at large, and by those closest to us that we must love and stay connected to our family members because "it's your family."

For those of us who are religious or spiritual, we may feel that strict religious instruction holds us hopelessly and erroneously stuck in relationships with our toxic family members. We may think or have even been told that God demands us to be endlessly patient and tolerant of the manipulations and abuses directed toward us. We come to believe that we're expected to stay in relationship with our toxic family no matter how poorly they treat us.

Is this really true? Are we supposed to remain with family members who have never loved us? And what if our family experience has been so hurtful and dysfunctional that we find ourselves in the position of only having one very painful and scary choice—to separate ourselves from our family permanently or continue to suffer their unrelenting abuse?

Are we bad people if we choose to separate ourselves from them?

Are we unholy and immoral if we establish no contact?

No, I believe we are not.

It's unfortunate and extremely painful that when we do finally gather the strength and courage to stand up to our toxic family members, we find ourselves being judged, scrutinized, and labeled as unloving, heartless, and cruel people. Why is it that so many spectators assume that because we have finally reached a point of having to set limits on the hurtful behavior of our toxic family members that this somehow equates to us no longer loving these people and even being unloving ourselves?

I am convinced that God is a loving God and that he would never require me to gain his love and approval by my allowing anyone, and I mean *anyone*, to cause me persistent emotional pain. This cannot have anything to do with God or love if God is loving. I cannot go along with the belief that, to be a person of value, I must tolerate just about any abuse brought my way. When people jump to this conclusion about God, not only does it lack logic, but it is also incredibly manipulative and shaming of the victim and, even worse, honors our perpetrators.

According to Sister Renee Pittelli, author of *The Christian's Guide to No Contact*, the Bible never tells us we must always forgive unrepentant people. Yet our abusers and their supporters will pull out all the stops to make us feel guilty for removing ourselves from their web of devastation. Many of the same people who have never experienced this type of toxic family abuse often cannot understand why we *have* to leave. Due to their frequent religious and spiritual misunderstandings, far too many of us suffer under their beliefs—beliefs that urge us to "hang in there" with our toxic family members, to give them nothing but our love and respect, claiming that if we just continue to be "good," our toxic family members will eventually begin to appreciate our kindness and start showing us the love we desire. The hard truth, however, is that we must come to accept that our toxic family members do not love or respond to goodness or kindness in the same ways that healthy people do.

Pittelli offers that many biblical passages, especially those found in Proverbs, teach us that our toxic family members will suffer the consequences of their behavior. The proverb "whoso rewardeth evil for good, evil shall not depart from his house"[25] shows us that there are people who will reward us for being kind to them by being evil to us. Our toxic family members do just this. They take advantage of our connection with them, of our vulnerability, and of our needs to have them be a significant part of our life. In the Bible, God instructs his children on how he wants them to relate to and live in peace with one another. Pittelli makes it clear that the Bible is not instructing the children of God on how to be "loving and forgiving toward, live in peace with, and maintain relationships with evil people."[26]

As children of God and survivors of toxic family abuse, we are to take up the full force of God and fight the dark forces, not peacefully coexist with them. It is our divine right to stand up to cruel and manipulative people. It is our right to expose their hurtful ways, confront them, and not allow them to continue to be abusive toward us.

If we do this with our parents, are we dishonoring them? Are we violating the biblical commandment to honor our parents (Exodus 20:12)? No, we are not. As Pittelli explains, all we are doing is giving up trying to change our toxic family members. In that way, we are honoring their choice to be the psychologically abusive people they want to be and to live as they wish. Moreover, Pittelli argues that we are helping our toxic parents not to sin anymore by removing ourselves from the picture so they can no longer inflict their emotional abuse upon us. Maintaining contact with them encourages them to continue abusing us by giving them a target. We are not doing anything cruel or dishonoring to them by simply staying away from them. Instead, we are helping them resist the temptation to be psychologically abusive, at least toward us.[27]

No contact also helps us stand up to our abusers in the best way, which is through the use of silence. Joel Osteen says if we cannot be positive, we can at least be quiet. If we don't have anything nice to say to our toxic family members, it is best to say nothing.

Still, some people will tell us that we need to be more patient with our toxic family, as if we haven't been patient enough. Some religiously inspired individuals will even tell us that we need to wait on God to change our situation, as if we play no role in directing our own lives. The truth of the matter is that, when the

Bible speaks about patience, it mostly refers to us not losing faith in God when we're going through challenging times. Patience in this context requires that we discipline ourselves to wait while God works things out and brings us solutions. While we're waiting, we must show God our fortitude and perseverance to demonstrate that we have absolute faith in him to take care of us.[28] Nevertheless, Pittelli helps us understand that the Bible is *not* teaching patience as a path to tolerate the abuses of our toxic family members. We are not to patiently wait for them to change, which they will not do anyway, and we are not to dismiss their cruelties as they repeatedly dish them out to us. God instructs us to leave relationships with wicked and evil people, to separate from them, to purge them from our midst.[29] We should never be patient with persistent evil!

Healing Moment

Our expectations for proper treatment and decency from the people in our lives are healthy.

Reality comes down to answering this question: Do our toxic family members really love us enough to work things out? The answer is no. When our toxic family members are confronted with the boundaries we place upon their behavior, they would rather end the relationship than assume any accountability for how they have treated us. What is so baffling to me as a psychologist is that I have never witnessed anyone choke or die over the following series of words: I am sorry, I was wrong, and you are right. However, I've seen many important relationships torn apart and absolutely destroyed because toxic family members would prefer to lose the relationship with us than to say any combination of those three simple statements. It is emotionally devastating to realize that we are this unimportant to them when compared to their obsession to take care of their own egos.

The large majority of us struggle and suffer for years, or even for our entire life, desperately trying every possible alternative to make leaving our toxic family dynamics unnecessary. Some of us wait until our mental and physical health is failing from the stress. Others of us hold off until our marriages or children are so adversely impacted by the toxic family members in our lives that leaving literally becomes a matter of survival.

Why do we struggle for so many years?

Because they're our family. No matter how awful, destructive, and selfish they are, no matter how much they terrorize us, they are still mother and father, brother and sister, grandmother and grandfather … our family.

Who do we turn to when our own family isn't there for us? When our family is the very source of our pain, isolation, mistrust, and fractured selves?

Healing Moment

 Eventually we will have no choice. It will either be us or them.

I had a moment while on a run where I felt utterly alone after finally cutting ties with my mother, the last tie to my nuclear family. A song came on by Bruno Mars called "Treasure." I realized in that moment that while my parents had forsaken me, I was not alone. I was God's daughter.

Lyric Therapy
Treasure, that is what you are
Honey, you're my golden star
You know you can make my wish come true
If you let me treasure you
—"Treasure," by Bruno Mars[30]

I knew, in the moment that this song came on, that I was treasured, that I would be taken care of, and that I was God's golden star.

I can also say, without a shadow of a doubt, that all my dreams have come true since getting all the negativity from my toxic family members out of my life. I have secured publishing contracts, met a wonderful man, feel loved by his family, have a strong network of friends who I consider my chosen family, have built my dream private practice, and have a huge family of Facebook followers who have joined my journey into healing. I help people in the way that I desperately needed when struggling through destructive family relationships. These are the rewards and miracles that have come to me since letting go of my toxic family members.

What I know now is that the people in my life who genuinely love and care about me will protect me, understand my decision-making, and support me to protect myself. Anyone who truly loves me would never, for even one second, want me to be subjected to the manipulation of the toxic family members toward whom I've chosen to establish silence. If anything, they will help me keep my boundaries up, firm, and tight.

In cutting ties, I have found that I am not alone. Nor am I without love and security.

Healing Moment

We all have stand-down moments that require us to stand up, stand in the center of ourselves, and know who we are.

—*Oprah Winfrey*

Healing MomentIt is promised to us in the Judeo-Christian Scriptures that who or whatever has caused us sorrow and pain will be replaced with healthy, loving relationships and other blessings that often come in the most unexpected ways and from the most unexpected places.[31] I have witnessed this in my own life and in the lives of those I treat. For example, I heard Joel Osteen tell a story about a woman who really wanted to meet the love of her life and get married. Osteen suggested that she make a list of all the things she wanted in a partner and to put that list in a picture frame and allow God time to bring her what she desired. He guaranteed this woman that, one day, a picture of the man she loved would soon replace the list she had made. I decided to follow the direction Osteen gave her since I didn't want to attract another toxic relationship. Each day I would kiss the tips of my fingers and touch the top of the frame that held my list. Soon I met a man who adores me and is healthy for me. I have since expanded this practice to all my goals. I can say that in having been offered a book contract for writing my story here has been the most profound example of what the Scriptures say. Being enabled to tell my story and through it help others, I feel that all the pain I have endured and continue to handle has and is coming full circle. Every evil done to me is being made up to me tenfold.

Healing Moment

"No weapon formed against you shall prosper,
And every tongue which rises against you in judgment
You shall condemn...," says the LORD.

—Isaiah 54:17

Getting to the place of receiving such gifts is a matter of working through our fears and finding the warrior within us to fight for what is right and true. God, more than anything, is a promoter and supporter of the truth. If we have the truth, and we share that truth with others as an offering of help or support, God will prosper us. When we go through feelings of fear and doubt, we must turn to examine the truth of our experience. Experience tells us that certain people are not ever going to change. This is a reality, and this is the reality we need to deal with when it comes to our toxic family members. The Bible clearly tells us that evil people—those who have hardened themselves to that which is good—do not change, not because they can't but because they won't.[32]

Misused and Abused Scriptures

The dominant religious heritage of America is Christianity, and its most important religious texts are compiled in the Bible. The set of books in the Bible, when rightly interpreted, provide a good deal of hope and help to those who have been victimized. Tragically, however, many biblical passages have been twisted to mean things that they don't really mean. And some of these passages have been used against those of us who have suffered abuse at the hands of our toxic family.

A Bible passage often used against us is this: "Take heed to yourselves: If thy brother trespass against thee, rebuke him; and if he repent, forgive him" (Luke 17:3). The rebuke part of the passage is usually ignored. What's emphasized is the call to forgive. Sister Pittelli teaches that our toxic family members (especially when they are religious) often misquote this text, using it to keep us down and in a state of oppression. They use the Bible to denigrate us when they tell us how it demands we forgive and forget, and that it instructs us not to hold grudges or forsake our family. They use this scriptural passage in particular to threaten us, claiming that if we don't forgive them, God will cast us away to live our lives in isolation. However, a closer look at this passage does not support our family members' take on it. These are Jesus' words, and he specifically tells us to rebuke the sinner and forgive him—*only if he repents*. Have we rebuked our toxic family members by voicing to them how poorly they have mistreated us? Yes, we have, and in too many ways to count. And have our toxic family members repented? No, they have not.

A fuller understanding of biblical teaching about repentance and forgiveness includes God's role in all of this. The Bible tells us to forgive as God has forgiven us.[33] He forgives us when we come to him and confess our wrongdoings, ask him for forgiveness, and repent (turn away from our bad behavior).[34] God does not forgive those who are 'stiff-necked,' who continue doing wrong, and who refuse to repent.[35] In other words, forgiveness, even from the God of the Bible, requires repentance from the person who needs the forgiveness.[36] Forgiveness is never granted carte blanche. And if repentance doesn't come, eventually punishment will, at least from God.[37]

And repentance is not simply mouthing the words "I'm sorry." Repentance requires confession—an acknowledgment of the wrongs done to the person wronged—*and* a turning away from the wrongs done. By turning away, the wrongdoer chooses to live differently, to act differently, to be different. In other words, the wrongdoer moves away from the path of wrongdoing and starts down the path of rightdoing because he sees this as the right thing to do.[38] If he doesn't do this, then repentance has not occurred, no matter what he says to the contrary.

Without genuine repentance, forgiveness should not be granted. This is because forgiveness is an act of mercy—an act that assumes that a real wrong has been done and that what it deserves is justice, not mercy or forgiveness. And justice demands payment or retribution for the injustice done. The most basic understanding of justice is that it is giving to another what is due. What is due to a wrongdoer is rebuke, correction, and, as needed, punishment. Mercy can be granted the wrongdoer, but when it is given, it is always given voluntarily. It is never deserved, and it cannot be rightly demanded or expected. And when mercy is offered and rejected, then justice kicks in and carries out the due consequences. A prime example of this comes through one of the parables Jesus told.

He spoke about a king who had slaves who were indebted to him. This king decided that he wanted to settle the slaves' financial accounts with him. One slave owed him more than fifteen years worth of a common laborer's wages. Since the slave could not repay the debt, the king ordered that the slave, his family, and their possessions be sold in an attempt to recoup as much of the debt as possible. The slave pleaded with the king to give him time to repay the debt. The king "felt compassion" for the slave, let him go, and forgave him the money due. This was an amazing act of undeserved kindness and mercy!

When the slave left the king's presence, he ran across one of his fellow slaves who owed him just a day's wages, grabbed him, choked him, and demanded that he repay all he owed. When the fellow slave begged him for more time to make payment on the debt, the forgiven slave refused and threw him into prison until he could pay off all the money due. Other slaves saw what happened and grieved over it. They reported to the king what the forgiven slave had done.

In response, the king recalled the forgiven slave and told him: "You wicked slave, I forgave you all that debt because you pleaded with me. Should you not also have had mercy on your fellow slave, in the same way that I had mercy on you?" Moved with justified anger, the king turned the cruel slave over to be tortured until he was able to pay off his huge debt.[39]

Notice that the king's initial feelings of compassion led him to forgive the slave's massive debt. And yet the slave's actions following this incredible act of mercy demonstrated how selfish and unforgiving he was, even toward someone who owed him far less money than he had owed the king. In effect, the forgiven slave took advantage of the mercy granted him to abuse someone he should have been kind toward. And the king's response was not to keep forgiving the ungrateful slave but to demand the fullness of justice from him. Mercy spurned deserved the consequences justice brings about.

Our toxic family isn't even as "humble" as the slave who begged the king to forgive his debt. They demand that we forgive them, and they don't even believe that they need forgiveness. They don't see themselves in our debt at all. But they are just as selfish, demanding, and ungrateful as the forgiven slave was. And like him, whatever mercy we offered them has been repeatedly rejected. All they ever deserved was justice for their countless offenses. Now with mercy spurned, justice is due them until their debts are fully paid—and pay them they will not, at least not voluntarily.

Healing Moment

 God does not expect more from us than he is willing to do.

Do we imagine ourselves to be higher than God? Since God requires full and genuine repentance before forgiveness is granted, so should we.

Although we are told in the Bible to love and pray for our enemies,[40] I want to make it clear that we are not told to continue to purposefully expose ourselves to their psychologically abusive ways as an act of noble love on our part. Even Jesus, the one who told us to pray for our enemies, refused to voluntarily entrust himself to individuals he distrusted.[41] Likewise, the most loving thing we can do for all involved is to stay away. If we continue in these relationships and allow the abuse to continue, we do our toxic family members no favors by assisting and rewarding their descent into becoming even more skilled abusers.

The Way Forward

We are each here in this life as unique individuals graced to own the rights to our personal freedom. The best thing we offer this world is to show up and be exactly who we are. Shannon Thomas teaches that "harm in the name of God must be called what it is: spiritual abuse through the misapplied application of scripture regarding forgiveness, divorce and acceptance of intolerable behavior. Churches and their leadership are not educated or prepared to recognize situations where the parties are personality disordered."[42]

When we are children, our God is our ultimate parent. If we have had the unfortunate experience to have toxic parents, it is our right to find the God who supersedes them.

We have the right to find a God who would love us enough to never guilt us into remaining in any relationship that is horribly unhealthy for us.

We need to find the God who would not use his Word to trap us and make us feel spiritually oppressed.

I do not believe that bondage is God ordained. Freedom is every individual's personal right with no one possessing the oppressive rights to rob us from God's greatest gift—our individuality and freedom.

When my father and my mother forsake me, then the LORD will take me up. (Psalm 27:10)

Lyric Therapy
I won't soothe your pain
I won't ease your strain
You'll be waiting in vain
I got nothing for you to gain
—"Eyes on Fire," by Blue Foundation[43]

11

Recovery

So much can be said about recovering from toxic family abuse. Among all the questions asked of me, one I hear all the time from people who are suffering is, *Why do I still care to even think or wonder about those who hurt me so much?* This is a good question, and it strikes at the heart of one of the most serious problems we face in our recovery from family abuse: We still care about our family because we hope to get something from them that they will never give us—a healthy sense of closure.

When we choose to leave our toxic family relationships, the recovery is different than when we leave a healthy relationship. Healthy relationships don't abuse us or mess with our head, our self-worth, or our self-concept. Only toxic relationship abuse does this. Recovery is hard because when we leave these toxic dynamics, we leave feeling completely lost to ourselves. We are left alone to try to find our way to reality.

A major part of our recovery is learning to pick up the pieces of our shattered identity and nurture them back to health. Recovering means we work through the poisoned layers of doubt and confusion that our toxic family have sown deeply in us—into the very fabric of how we perceive ourselves and others. We have to let go of the desire to feel heard, loved, and understood by them. They will never give us this kind of closure. This is incredibly challenging for us to accept because it seems that it should be easy and natural to find common ground with those we love and to feel understood. Our recovery will entail education more than anything else. We're not sick enough to understand our enemy, so we must learn about them in books, articles, therapy, online support groups, and other places. Once we begin to understand what we're dealing with, we have clarity that we were not, are not, and never could have been the sole problem in their lives or the sole cause of the demise of our relationship with them.

Healing Moment

 It is not hard to determine *if* someone is toxic. It is hard to *accept* that someone is toxic.

Hope as Dope

We cannot remove ourselves from our toxic family members if we use hope as dope. Hope is a wonderful thing when it is not misused as a treacherous form of denial. Hoping our toxic family members will eventually turn into good people is not healing. This belief keeps us in the one-down position, with the problem solely in our hands to fix. We cannot fix someone's insides with our outsides. Hope is of no help in this arena. H. G. Tudor in his book *Manipulated* teaches that our toxic family members use our empathic nature of trying to see the good in everyone as a tool to keep us attached to them and under their control. The large majority of us are eternal optimists who believe that love can conquer all and that there is not a human being out there who cannot be saved. This viewpoint is what keeps us attached to our toxic family members, hoping they will change, hoping that with enough information they will see the error of their ways, hoping they will have a moment of revelation over why they have treated us so poorly, and hoping they will recognize exactly why they need to change. Our hope for these things keeps us clinging to our abusive family. It ensures that we will try harder to please them. It leads us to dare not leave them in case things actually get better. Because of our hope, we do not want to give up. Giving up makes us the bad guy, and it goes against our morals and good nature. We do not want to risk losing the fantasy of what it would be like to be loved by a healthy family. This is why hope is such a powerful emotion and exactly why our toxic family members exploit it for their joy and our demise.

To heal we must examine ourselves and our own vulnerabilities. This type of examination is incredibly important because of how much we learn about ourselves through it. It's not about refusing to ever be vulnerable again. Rather, it's about examining those people who have manipulated and exploited our vulnerabilities. The more we study our enemy, the more wisdom we develop and the more equipped we are to make decisions that work to benefit our mental and emotional health. It's up to us to protect ourselves and determine who is healthy and who is not before giving our heart again. We must be brave enough to take our blinders off and look at what *is* so we can make the life-changing decisions we need to recover and find the true happiness we seek. We must surrender to the idea that our healing will always be an inside job. There is no amount of healing we can get from another person that will sustain us long-term. When we're stuck in toxic family ties, the tendency is to base our happiness and healing on our toxic family members changing and coming to understand and admit the errors in how they treated us. Yet happiness, freedom, and fulfillment will never come if we choose to believe our healing can happen in this way. This path is truly a dead end.

Dedication to the Truth

Is it possible to fully recover from toxic relationship abuse? Yes, it is!

Does the pain ever fully go away? The acute pain does, but the memory of it forever remains. And that's a good thing. Pain creates memories for the purpose of making sure we never forget what happened to us. When we get manipulated, we remember. The pain that comes from being manipulated is a warning, signaling us that something wrong and bad has happened. These memories help us become more aware and alert going forward.

Part of recovering is training ourselves to follow our instincts (what we feel inside) and examine the facts (the abusive ways in which our family treated us.) Look at it this way: if we touch a hot stove and burn ourselves, we will always think about stoves as something that we must be careful around because they can burn us if we're not careful. This is called wisdom. The process is the same after we cut ties with our toxic family members. They burned us over and over, so we will always have a link back to them that reminds us of the pain they have caused.

There's another comparison we can draw here. Just as the stove doesn't care that it burned us, neither do our toxic family members care that they've hurt us. We must not worry if we find ourselves thinking about them ten, twenty, or thirty years from now. When something hurts us, we remember. And we're smart to remember. Remembering is fundamental to survival. But what we commit to memory matters. We must commit to remembering our toxic family abuse from a place of objectivity rather than with a false longing. In other words, we must not let a burn from a stove make us never want to cook again. Likewise, just because we've had toxic relationship pain doesn't mean we live our life so terrified that we never open up again to others. Of course, we just never again open ourselves to our toxic family members. Nevertheless, each day we live afraid and avoid love, we allow the experience of our abusive family to starve us of love and life, which gives them the win. Recovery means that we learn from the experiences we've had so we can make better choices in the future.

The emotional pain we have experienced from our toxic family members is a useful guide when opening our hearts to other people. What we learn in our recovery shows us exactly how, when, and why *we* abandoned ourselves to make another person happy. It teaches us about the unhealthy patterns of behavior we need to work through to become whole and healthy. All of the pain we have experienced is beneficial toward our growth so we must try not to resist it when we're in it. We must be brave enough to surrender to it, learn from it, and accept the truth of it.

Once we have the truth, we can heal. We must stay dedicated to the truth of our experience to avoid the predators of fear and doubt that make us vulnerable once again to the abuses of our toxic family and open our hearts to other toxic people. It is not a fun truth to hold, that our toxic family members are who they are and how they are. It's painful. I have cried, sobbed, and screamed many tears, fearing that they would never come to an end. I have never wanted a truth to be more different than the truth of the manipulative ways my toxic family members operate. Each time when I've been deep in that type of pain, I have always asked myself, *Why am I not lovable? What is so wrong with me that I am not lovable?* This is not how children should feel during or after their childhood. But until we accept how poisonous our abusers have been—until we accept the truth about them—we will never learn from and move beyond the terrible damage they caused.

Healing Moment

 In our recovery, a dedication to truth means we focus on saving ourselves by paying more attention to what our toxic family members do rather than what they say. The truth is always better told through actions than words.

Learning to Trust Our Instincts

A big part of our recovery is learning to trust what we feel inside to be true. This is extremely challenging because we've been trained to discount what we feel all throughout our childhood. We have learned to feel guilty for what we feel because everything looked good on the outside. Because our family life appeared good to everyone else, we blame ourselves for not having the correct feelings about our lives and our family members. I have had many people say to me, "Your mom is so great!" while all I think inside is, *She's not great to me.* I figured I felt this way because there was something wrong with *me* rather than something wrong with the way she treated me. If a person doesn't know my mother deeply, he would never know what it was like for me to live with her.

I recently watched the movie *Lady Bird,* and the toxic dynamic shared between the mother and Lady Bird was like watching my own life in so many ways. Even the way the mother treated her husband and adoptive son were deeply similar to what I grew up with. In one scene, Lady Bird is so frustrated with her mother's passive-aggressive jabs that she literally launches herself out of a moving car. I know what that fury feels like. I have lived it and raged it. And I've been called abusive for it. I was made to believe that I was the problem, that my reaction to my mother's abuse was the abuse being perpetuated. There is no path to developing self-confidence when nothing about who we are is ever validated.

Lindsey Gibson, author of *Adult Children of Emotionally Immature Parents*, explains that our toxic family members are too self-consumed to think or know how to validate the feelings and instincts of their children. Without this validation, children learn to give in to what others seem sure about. When we have been raised to feel worthless, we expect the same from other people in our adult lives. We enter the world of love and relationships with such little confidence that we have a hard time believing that others could be genuinely interested in us. Because of this, we are too afraid to ask for what we need from others. We fear rejection. To us, rejection from others only proves our toxic family members must have been right about us. We have been programmed to believe that having needs of our own bothers other people, so we don't ask for what we need and end up stifling ourselves by constantly acquiescing to others to stay in relationships we don't even want to be in. In this way we end up perpetuating the emotional loneliness we were raised in.

Out of our insecurities, we strive to be needless in relationships. We take on the belief that we are the person who has to do all the work because *who could possibly love us if we're not the person doing all the work*. We have learned we don't deserve love. We have learned we have to work hard for it. We know that if anyone is going to be wrong or needs to change, it will, without a doubt, end up being us. This is a horrible way to be in a relationship because if the relationship fails, due to no fault of our own, we interpret relationship failures as *we* didn't do enough and that *we* are, in truth, fundamentally unlovable.

When I have been in toxic friendships or romantic relationships, to which there were many while as I was trying to heal, I would rationalize why I had to try so hard. The only thing I've ever known is that it's normal to struggle daily to get along with the people closest to me. I teach my patients who have developed the same pattern that, while a certain amount of work is absolutely necessary to maintain communication and closeness in our relationships, it should not feel like an unrewarding and unrelenting daily climb up Mount Everest. The truth is, if both partners in a relationship love each other, understand each other's feelings, and are positive and supportive toward each other, relationships are primarily pleasurable and not arduous. We are not asking too much to desire to feel even the most general sense of happiness when we see the people we love and care for. We want to look forward to sharing our time with them.

As we recover, we start trusting ourselves to know when we are emotionally satisfied and feeling valued. We can trust ourselves to know when someone is giving us full-measure. Having healthy needs and being needy are fundamentally different. We are not a bottomless pit of needs, as our parents have made us feel. Gibson ensures us that we can trust the prompts from our instincts that tell us when something we need to feel loved is missing in our relationships and to find the words to communicate this to others.

Common Emotional Issues

Being at odds with or disconnected from our families doesn't serve us in a way that we'd like. Nearly all of us would prefer a different situation, one where we could feel that sense of safety and connection in our familial bonds. To have to disconnect from them alters every part of our lives. So we must not doubt for one minute that to go at our lives all alone takes a strong warrior. We will have internal battles to contend with after separating from them, but at least we will not be around them for one re-injury after another, never letting us have enough time and space to work toward our recovery.

In my own personal healing and in the work I've done with patients over the last nearly thirty years, I have come to understand that we have the following core wounds to heal once we separate from our toxic family members.

Low Self-Worth

Danu Morrigan teaches that the reason our toxic family members impact us throughout our lives is because they are responsible for programming our beliefs. We respond automatically based on the core beliefs we were raised on. It makes logical sense then that, when we are loved well as children, we gather that evidence and conclude that we are valuable, lovable, and worthwhile. If, however, we were not loved enough and we were consistently neglected and shamed, we draw conclusions from that evidence too: We were not loved by our toxic family members because we were not lovable; we were neglected because we weren't worth taking care of; and we were humiliated because we are shameful.

Healing Moment

The brain can be fooled. This is the very reason our toxic family members succeeded in confusing us about who we are and who they are. If our brain as young, developing children always accurately knew realty, our toxic family members never would have been able to so thoroughly persuade us that their version of who we are was the correct one.

Recovery is what happens when we begin to see who the real problem was in our lives, from whom the sickness really came.

Children are innocent. We are not born with low self-worth. We are raised with it. It doesn't benefit a child to have cruel, immature parents. As adults we must work to detox our core beliefs of our family members' lies and trust the reality of what we know to be true, regardless of the multitude of denials and false stories our family members spoke to keep us weak, quiet, and confused. The last thing they want to face is the truth of who they really are. The best way toxic parents keep their secrets is to dominate and control their children into feeling too afraid, confused, and guilty to tell the truth.

Suffer from Perfectionism

Many of us suffer from a sensitivity to, not a rejection of, criticism. Because we've been criticized our entire lives—told that we're too sensitive, too difficult to please, too hard to get along with—it can be hard for us, even as adults, to take in healthy or honest feedback from others. Healthy feedback is enough to put us into deep distress, defensiveness, and fears of abandonment. We immediately feel wrong and bad and mostly end up getting defensive instead of being open because we feel attacked and afraid. The little lies our toxic parents told us about ourselves brainwash us into holding false beliefs about who we are and what we do.

In an effort to overcompensate for what we falsely believe to be permanent flaws in our character, many of us strive to be absolutely perfect. We try to get perfect grades, graduate, and attain post-graduate degrees, play the right sports, wear the right clothes, never argue, and never state an opinion of ours if it goes against another's. To be perfect, we think we must agree to go along with what others want.

Fear People

When we grow up under volatile, immature, chaotic, and selfish family members, we are nurtured to believe that people are scary and cruel. And when we are raised to question our lovability and worth, how can we trust that others will see us as worthy? Because conflict was so high growing up in our toxic family, many of us learned to agree with the poisonous dynamics as a way to find or keep the peace. We may have also lived our lives trying to please and prove our value to our parents.

Healing Moment

Children should not have to audition or "try out" for parental love, attention, or approval.

Rage or Shut Down

When we see our parents mishandling their emotions, especially the emotions of rage or martyrdom, children come to develop a malignant form of disrespect for their parents. Parents are supposed to be our justice system—one that is fair, stable, and consistent. When our parents mismanage their own emotions, we do not perceive that they can handle our behavior; rather, we come to believe they cannot handle their own. This is why so many children who come from toxic families rage when around their parents and when experiencing the manipulative games they play. Our parents create the rage we feel. But we get punished and ostracized for it, which eventually leads us to shut down all together.

We will often carry this same pattern into relationships outside of our toxic families. I used to struggle with rage, and now, when I am in conflict with someone I love, I tend to shut down completely. Once I am in this mode, it is difficult to find the words I need to speak. I now understand that I need a little alone time to work through the emotional flooding I feel when I am in this place. Time to examine my reaction helps me find the clarity I need to communicate. I am happy I have developed this skill. I have learned that not everything I feel needs to be communicated right away. It's okay to tell others I need to take a moment to digest what I am feeling before I communicate.

Fear We're Unlovable

Because we've been raised in gaslighting, projection, guilt, deflection, and outright lies where every aspect of our emotional life has been denied and invalidated, we were left feeling that we are not lovable. There is nothing more hopeless or treacherous than feeling fundamentally unwanted and unlovable. It is a pain too large for children to process because we're so busy needing to view our parents as good and responsible that we believe that if there are problems, we are the cause, not our parents. They are not wrong or unlovable—we are. And because we need them desperately as children, we feel a gut-wrenching emptiness and overwhelming shame over how horrible and worthless we are. When we believe this at our core, this hole in our heart takes a lifetime of recovery. This old belief sneaks up on us each time we feel rejected. When it comes up for me, I make room for it and re-parent my way through it. How I talk to myself is the most important language in my healing. I talk to this feeling and address it as a healthy parent would. I tell it exactly what I would tell my daughter if she were feeling the same way.

Prone to Cling or Run

Because we had no balance in our emotional worlds growing up, when we start developing other relationships in life, our insecurities create us into runners or clingers. I have actually been both in my life.

When I was younger, I was clingy. I couldn't imagine that someone could really love or like me so I would cling to them. I was always worried about people rejecting or abandoning me, and it was this irrational fear of mind that drove people away from me. The more distant someone became, the more I would cling. When we're clingy, we're unconsciously searching for people to love us and fill us in the ways our toxic family members never did.

As I have matured, I have become more of a runner. If I start sensing things aren't right in a relationship and I feel I've done my best to express myself and there is still no understanding with my partner, I start to run. I start to feel that if I can't be understood on something not all that deep, then my partner will have a really hard time understanding me when things become more significant and intense. I falsely interpret this to mean that I am a burden, so I unconsciously start preparing for plan B.

Tend to Make Poor Relationship Choices

Like it or not, we tend to pick relationships that are very similar in their dynamics to our toxic family situation. Until we heal, it is normal to find ourselves in toxic or one-sided relationships, not because we mean to but because they are familiar. We end up repeating our cycle over and over, which only increases the disconnection we feel to the good in ourselves, in other people, and in life as a whole. I cannot tell you how many people, my patients and me included, who had someone in their lives who was too nice to them, and because this kindness was unfamiliar, it made us so uncomfortable that we terminated the relationship. I treated a woman who knew that her unhealthy love relationship patterns had to change because she was afraid that she wouldn't be sexually attracted to someone who was nice to her. How sad is that?

Lindsay Gibson shows that there are many good reasons why the past repeats itself.[44] The most primitive parts of our brain tell us that safety lies in familiarity.[45] We unconsciously gravitate toward relationships and situations that are familiar to us because we know how to deal with them. As children, we don't recognize, or at least we don't want to acknowledge, the flaws in our parents, because seeing them as flawed or substandard is scary. But by denying the painful truth about our parents, we aren't able to recognize similarly hurtful people in our future relationships. This form of denial or lack of the ability to recognize the pattern causes us to experience the same painful heartbreak over and over. We just don't see it coming, even when all the signs are right before us. Instead, we keep believing that things will be different each next time, but the different doesn't come.

Need Validation and Understanding

One of the greatest challenges that stands in opposition to our healing is the need to feel validated, appreciated, and understood by those we love. What we all suffer from in coming from toxic families is a disenfranchised grief. We live with a grief that is not accepted or validated by society. Loss is one of the most common experiences that brings about grieving. Although this is often viewed as normal, there are times when grieving is disqualified. Cutting ties with one's family members is one of those instances. Traditional forms of grief are more widely accepted, such as when a parent dies. When grief is not accepted but rather viewed as something we brought on ourselves, there are few, if any, support systems to help us cope with our disenfranchised grief. Hardly anyone will validate a child's experience over that of a parent's. Because so many people falsely assume that all parents love and treat their children well, many children go unheard and disbelieved. Instead, we are told to change who we are so our parents will be less angry. Then we are promised that life will be "good" for us. But in a toxic family, a child's cooperation only further fuels parental manipulation. The "good" never arrives.

Dr. Larry Nassar was a physician for the American gymnastics team. During his career, he sexually abused hundreds of women who were supposed to be cared for by him. He was eventually arrested, tried, convicted, and sentenced to up to 175 years in prison. As I watched the Larry Nassar case in the media, I felt so happy these young women and men got to have their day in court with the evil person who raped them. I was particularly struck by Kyle Stephen's testimony because her parents didn't believe her when she told them what Larry had been doing to her. When she talked about her parents in her testimony, I could feel the hurt, betrayal, and abandonment she felt. These outcomes were also mine. I could tell that Kyle could recover more easily from the physical acts Nassar so vilely did to her more than she would be able to recover from the emotional abandonment he created between her and her parents who rejected her. Kyle's parents wanted her to apologize to Nassar, just as our parents want us to apologize to them.

Rather than accepting Kyle as the victim, she became the family scapegoat. Her parents found it easier to believe a well-known doctor than their own child, even though she stood to benefit nothing from telling her parents what had happened to her. Similarly, people nearly always believe seemingly well-to-do parents over their children because, well, "kids will be kids."

If you grew up in an *emotionally* toxic family where abandonments and cruelties had no physical evidence you could point to, you experienced emotional rape. Unlike Nassar's victims who underwent physical assault, emotional rape is almost impossible to prove. And as a child, adults are less likely to believe you when you make claims against your parents.

Larry Nassar, like our toxic family members, didn't want to hear the testimony of the girls he abused, and he even penned a letter to the judge about how he wasn't wrong and wasn't mentally fit enough to withstand their testimony. He didn't want to hear these girls for the same reasons our parents don't want to hear us: They do not want to have to take any accountability for their actions. This is the reason my mother didn't read the first book I wrote. She claimed it would be too hard *on her.* My father and brother used my book as their excuse to completely discard me from their lives. My toxic family members are really no different than Nassar. They didn't pen a letter to me, but their actions spoke loudly and clearly.

Still, there's one thing Nassar's victims received that I will not. They had their day in court while I never will.

I will never see my toxic family members face emotional rape charges because my rape isn't provable or visible.

I will never have a group of sisters to stand with me against the manipulation I withstood.

I will never have a judge to show belief, support, or compassion for me.

I will never have parents come so strongly to my defense that they want to physically harm those who have hurt me because my parents were my perpetrators.

And I will never have the support of an entire movement, #Metoo.

But I have experienced therapists who unknowingly contributed to my abuse, and I have had many adults, teachers, and coaches treat me as less than others or as a charity case because I just wasn't a "good kid." I was someone people could throw away because they believed my family members' smear job and decided I was angry, raging, failing, and acting out.

Why didn't anyone think, *What is going on in this little girl's life to make her so angry and hurt?*

The grief of being emotionally abused is invisible and vague, and, like Larry Nassar, our parents could covertly sling this abuse at us in front of others, provoke us to react, and then call us crazy. The laypeople who were present couldn't see the covert abuse or pick up on it. So to them, we did, in fact, look crazy.

Psychological abuse is a type of abuse that is secretive. It is mired deeply into our unique personal sensitivities that our parents created in us, but these are not noticeable to the public. We know we're being abused, but we can't prove it.

Healing Moment

Reactive abuse happens when a toxic person intentionally abuses someone. The victim responds with anger or another normal reaction, and the toxic abuser accuses the victim of being the abusive person.

When we finally get to a place where we decide to love ourselves enough to remove these toxic family members from our lives, we are not applauded, hugged, supported, and congratulated for our bravery, like Larry Nassar's victims were. Instead, more often than not, people will say, "But it's your family," and the abuse and emotional loneliness will continue. Shannon Thomas explains that emotional abuse and manipulation are among the most hidden injustices of our time because they leave their victims unable to trust even themselves. It is as if their lives are being violently shaken, like one would shake a snow globe where everything is always swirling in chaos.

So I am here to tell you that you are not alone. We are a vast group of people who often suffer in silence. Sharing this information is our collective day in court. All we have to do is find each other and speak out. Our stories of heroism are important to tell because the abuses we've endured have been cruel, unfair, and unrecognized. Taking this step of courage will be hard. When we don't have a Larry Nassar to blame and our parents take no accountability, we may unconsciously turn on ourselves by no fault of our own. We may take on the responsibility and blame that we do not deserve, thereby acting unjustly toward ourselves. But we must reinforce to ourselves the truth of our situation and refuse to indict ourselves. We cannot heal and get better if we continue to turn on ourselves and doubt what we know is true. We need to tell our stories, whether other people will accept them or not.

Lyric therapy

Out of the ashes, I'm burning like a fire
You can save your apologies, you're nothing but a liar
I've got shame, I've got scars, that I will never show
I'm a survivor, in more ways than you know
—"Warrior," by Demi Lovato[46]

12

The Healing Process

As we recover, we start to remember and connect with who we really are. We start connecting with the image of that amazing person we always thought or hoped we had the potential to be.

As I have moved farther away from my toxic family members, I have come to more deeply understand, accept, and embrace all that has happened to me. I am no longer confused, and I no longer doubt where the problem lies. This clarity has set me on the path to my long-term healing.

If we pull the word *remember* apart and make it *re-member* and then apply it to the healing process, we can see we left our childhoods emotionally dismembered, with our thoughts and feelings scattered all over the place. *Re-membering* means we are in the process of gathering our dismembered pieces and are putting ourselves back together into a cohesive whole. This type of healing is not an event. It's a lifelong process. It is difficult to reconnect to our personal power after it has been stolen from us or never given to us. The surest way to stay committed and thriving as we heal is to remain silent with those we have so bravely protected ourselves from. Silence is the line in the sand that indicates where we start and our toxic family members stop. This boundary allows us the space to heal what is hurt and lonely inside.

Emotionally Homeless

Keeping this boundary in place is not easy, however, no matter how much we need it. In fact, the greatest temptation we have going through our lives without our toxic family members is the risk of going back for the hope of the "fantasy family."

After I had cut the final ties to my toxic family members, I felt free but terrified. I felt emotionally homeless, as if I was freefalling into a void. As I have spent time recovering, I realize that I didn't feel any less emotionally homeless when I was fully engaged in my toxic family system. In fact, the pain and loneliness I felt then was much worse than what I feel now because I know that my emotional homelessness is my choice. I chose it—not my toxic family. *I* cut ties with *them*. Being untethered from all I knew about love and family didn't hurt me as much as it scared me. The newfound freedom felt strange. To continue in my healing, I stayed connected to my therapist, I held tightly to my daughter and my duties as her mother, and I kept close to my friends, my career, my business coach, my exercise routine, and the man and his family who came into my life after my decision to leave my toxic family was already made. All of these elements combined offered me the structure I needed to harness and soothe the feelings of freefalling and the anxiety that goes along with that.

I love the saying that time heals all wounds. I can say for myself and for many of my patients that, as time goes on, our wounds do start healing, our resilience and knowledge increase, and we deepen in who we are as people. I have come to realize since breaking free of my toxic family members that I was justifying insanity to stay connected with them. The longer I am free of their manipulations, I notice that more memories surface of instances of manipulation I didn't even have the time to focus on at the time they were happening because the next manipulation was already in play. Now I can see that even the smallest things that were going on or that were said to me all served to push me down. This new, uninterrupted quiet time away from their poison has given me the opportunity to think rationally about what I have had to endure. It feels good to be and act rationally rather than fearfully.

When I first cut ties with my family, part of the fear I experienced was the new sense of quiet in my life. At first the quiet was almost so deafening that it frightened me. I have come to understand it like this: If I had had a parent who smoked cigarettes while pregnant with me, I would have been born addicted to nicotine. At my birth, my body would have lost its consistent supply of nicotine, and I would have gone through a period of severe withdrawal as my body adjusted to living without this drug. Toxic family abuse is similar. The consistent hypervigilance we felt as we were manipulated and toyed with throughout our lives was our normal. When we are old enough and well enough to separate ourselves from our family's poison, we naturally go through a period of emotional withdrawal. We have to learn to live without the familiar and consistent rush of our own fight-or-flight emotions and the neurochemicals they produce. We have been raised to pair abuse and our responses to it with the concepts of love and attachment. It takes time and courage for us to finally go through detox and come out on the other side so we can see and experience life differently—life free of the poison that held us in its grip for so long.

Living without the familiarity of our toxic family members and all the pain, chaos, and drama they created is a difficult and sometimes confusing transition. Recovery turns the emotional volume down and allows us to live our lives more directly and with a deeper sense of simplicity. We have to work on our personal growth—on planting new roots deep into our own psychological earth. We have to recover our self-worth. Complete separation and time away allow us to recover and to remember—perhaps even finally establish—how to express who we really are. We are people who are deserving of love, good fortune, and acceptance. We cannot get to this point in our recovery if we don't let our toxic family members go and focus on healing ourselves. As adults, we are allowed to stop drinking their poison.

Healing Moment

We must do all we can not to let our toxic family members keep us afraid of love or life. The greatest "revenge" we have is moving on into new and healthier relationships where we receive love in all the ways they chose not to give it.

Our toxic family will never be brought up on charges and found guilty in a courtroom. But we can effectively arrest their abuse and bring upon them at least some of what they really deserve—isolation, the only form of prison we will ever get for them. In the toxic family dynamic, justice comes in the form of giving our toxic family members the natural consequences to come from their abuse of us. Just as bad people don't usually reform just because they are behind bars, our toxic family members won't reform just because they have been isolated from us—the ones they once controlled. However, their ability to abuse us has been curtailed. The attention they crave is no longer allowed, not from us anyway. In this way some justice has been meted out.

But it's not enough to move away from the source of what has poisoned our lives. We need to move toward something—the something we should have received from our parents but never did. We need genuine, heartfelt, abiding love. The kind of love that seeks for the true good of the beloved. Love is more than words, though not less. Love is action, behavior. Love works for the good of others. Love is not selfish but other-centered.[47] Yes, we can love ourselves, and we should too. But when someone says to us, "I love you," that needs to come through actions that strive to secure what is good for us, not what is destructive.

So how will we know for sure when what we have found is love? When love is real, there is very little insecurity about the other person, their intentions toward us, or their treatment of us. If others inadvertently treat us poorly, we can trust they had a good intention, that they will own their mistakes, and that they will take the actions necessary to avoid hurting us like that again. Healthy relationships bring us a sense of peace and comfort we haven't seen experienced anywhere else in our lives. There are no games, triangulations, scapegoating, lying, hiding, gaslighting, or two-facing. Backstabbing, jealousy, and gossip are absent. There are no teams fighting against us. When love is present, our efforts are supported, our accomplishments are celebrated, and our heart is valued as an undeniable treasure. When we fail in life, we are not laughed at, put-down, or condemned, and the one who says he or she loves us does not feel a sense of joy in watching us go through a hard time. When there are disagreements, there is no yelling or never-ending, brain-twisting arguments. When true love is present, so are vulnerability, open communication, feedback, apologies, and room for transformation and growth.

Love is kind and thoughtful.

Love is easy.

There is no chaos or drama.

There is no "making up."

There is respect.

There is time for one's self.

We are not flooded by another person's demands that can never be met.

We are allowed to be ourselves and are loved for exactly who we are.

We no longer feel emotionally homeless.

Healing Moment

 We were never "too sensitive." Perhaps, however, we were intuitive and saw the abuse we endured for the manipulation and cruelty that it was.

What about Forgiveness?

Inevitably, the topic of forgiveness comes up when abuse is discussed. Forgiveness is a confusing topic when we've been psychologically abused or neglected. I've read and heard a lot on this topic that blames the victim if she doesn't forgive. The reality is, life brings about painful experiences that are simply inexcusable, unjustifiable, and irreconcilable. Yet many theories around forgiveness teach that not to forgive another person is a form of self-punishment and may even be immoral. Our lack of forgiveness comes to be viewed as an offense we perpetrate against the individuals who hurt us.

I agree it is not healthy to harbor hateful, angry, and depressed feelings for a lifetime against who harmed us. On the other hand, I believe we can be in a place of unforgiveness and still be healthy and happy. I think there are five myths about forgiveness that hold us back and can even, at times, perpetuate our abuse.

Myth 1: Not forgiving persecutes the victim

On this view of forgiveness, if someone does something reprehensible to us, the burden of responsibility for healing switches over to the victim who now must forgive the perpetrator in order for any healing to occur. We are taught that if we don't forgive, then we, as the victim, are somehow morally flawed, and we have made ourselves incapable of moving on in an emotionally healthy way.

In truth, this myth shifts the burden away from the perpetrator and places it on the victim. The victim, not the perpetrator, is now held responsible for repairing the relationship and the damage done. At best, this lessens the perpetrator's responsibility and puts all the moral pressure on the victim. If the victim then delays in offering forgiveness or denies it altogether, then moral judgment falls on her and the perpetrator gets off the moral hook and may be treated as the victim!

When my mother has been caught and confronted on her abusive and spiteful ways, she falls into a pathetic heap of sobbing hysterics, ranting and martyring on and on about how she didn't mean to "hurt anyone," it's "always" all her fault, she just "can't do or say anything right," and I have "no idea how many hours" she spends in "self-loathing." In behaving this way, she very slyly dumps all of these dramatic emotions onto me, thereby deflecting away from the horrible thing she said or did that caused *me* pain. She places the responsibility for the consequences of her manipulative behavior and her unhappiness onto me. If I fail to forgive her and make her feel better because she feels so bad, I am considered mean. This is emotional abuse. It doesn't require forgiveness but exposure for what it is. And if forgiveness is offered, it will only embolden the perpetrator in her destructive ways and further her persecution of us, the victims.

The perpetrators must be held accountable, and forgiveness will not accomplish that.

Another problem with this myth about forgiveness is that it misunderstands whom forgiveness is for. The focus of forgiveness is not the victim but the perpetrator—in our case, those in our family who have abused us. Forgiveness is for their sakes, not for us. We grant them mercy for the wrongs they have done to us. We give them favor—and undeserved favor at that! For them to receive this mercy, they need to acknowledge that they have wronged us and demonstrate a commitment to changing their ways with us. This will be hard work on their part. And if they engage in it, they will actually participate in their own healing. Would we benefit from this radical change in their character and behavior? Of course we would. But that benefit would be secondary. Forgiveness is for the perpetrator's healing, not so much for ours. We would still need to do the hard work of healing our own lives regardless of what our abusers did or failed to do.

Now let's ask the central question: Can we expect our abusers to change in these positive ways? Can we count on them to engage in true repentance? No, and we would be unwise to do so. Hope would become our dope, all over again, and we would be hoovered back into the family system designed to manipulate us and hurt us, not to love us and care for us. Forgiveness, not unforgiveness, would end up re-crushing us.

Myth 2: Nothing is unforgivable

Really? There's nothing so heinous, so despicable, so inhumane, so horrific that forgiveness should not cover it? It seems to me that this makes light of the crimes committed. It also seems to demand that victims must forgive those who worked so relentlessly to destroy their lives. After all, if nothing is unforgivable, then all must be forgiven, at least that's what most people conclude when they accept this myth.

I reject this view. If forgiveness takes place, if it is real, it must be voluntary, and it must take into account and acknowledge the true depravity of what it is being offered for. Forgiveness cannot be demanded; it can only be granted. And if it is granted, it is a sign of mercy, for the perpetrator deserves only justice for the damage he or she has caused.

From my perspective, there are things that have been done to us that are inhumane and unforgivable. Acknowledging this is not wrong. It is simply affirming reality.

But you may come from a moral or religious viewpoint that calls on you to forgive no matter what has been done to you. If this is so and you feel strongly that you must comply, then consider forgiving the wrongdoer quietly and privately—that is, in your heart—but not to the abuser's face. Toxic family members will see expressions of forgiveness as weaknesses to exploit. Don't give in to their tactics this way. If you need to forgive them for your own healing, then do it, but keep it to yourself.

Myth 3: Forgiveness makes us "righteous"

Because we do not want to look bad in the eyes of others or be looked down upon within our spiritual or religious belief system, sometimes we forgive outwardly because we feel like we have to. We need to at least appear as if we are acting rightly. And some promoters of this myth will even tell us that if we keep acting as if we have forgiven our abuser, we will gradually make that forgiveness a reality in our lives. But you and I know that this isn't true. Inside we are still angry and flooded with feelings of rage, grief, depression, and helplessness. The more we force ourselves to forgive, the more this internal battle grows and the worse we feel. This is called "faking good," and it is a deadly form of denial. Faking good may outwardly help protect us from the ignorant judgments of others, but it doesn't help us heal inwardly, where it counts most.

Myth 4: A lack of forgiveness places us in an emotional prison

If we don't forgive, we are doomed to live miserable lives—so say a number of "authorities." We are shamed for the natural feelings we have. Isn't it normal to feel hurt, anger, anxiety, fear, depression, and a host of other emotions over what has been perpetrated against us? And yet, if we have these naturally occurring feelings and express them, we are given the clear message that all we are doing is giving our perpetrators power they don't deserve and, in the process, we are only hurting ourselves.

What this myth causes in us is self-punishment. We are made to feel guilty or weak for feeling what is only natural. In reality, there are things that have happened to us that may always trigger feelings of hurt or anger when we think about them. But to be told we are responsible for making someone else powerful with our naturally occurring feelings only makes us feel inadequate, and it forces us away from our grieving process. This forcing away of our feelings only creates what we're trying to avoid: a constant state of anger. In trying to keep our power, we end up losing our power.

I have had many people ask me, "Why would you give your family members the power to make you go silent?" My question back to them is, "How is it that you believe I am giving my toxic family members power because I've made the decision to protect myself?" My decision is coming from courage and strength, not from withering away out of weakness or fear. I challenge those who question me to see if they would have the courage it takes to be alone in the world without family. I do not feel I am surrendering any of my personal power to my toxic family members by choosing to stay away from them. I don't view my desire to wisely protect myself as a weakness, nor do I view succumbing to their abuse as a strength or a method of not giving them power. I simply refuse to keep toxic people in my life and choose not to guilt myself over this. I do not live my life feeling bitter, and I do not feel burdened or emotionally weak out of any hatred of them. I don't hate my toxic family members. Hating them would give them power over me. I simply feel relief that I no longer have to cope with the persistent pressures of being scapegoated, hurt, and manipulated by them.

Myth 5: Forgiveness requires reconciliation

With this myth forgiving involves us starting fresh with whomever we have forgiven. In other words, forgiveness requires relational reconciliation.

This is not true, nor is reconciliation always wise or healthy. In the situation of toxic family abuse, reconciliation is tantamount to subjecting ourselves to more abuse, which only further empowers the abuser while it continues to threaten our survival. If forgiveness is offered, reconciliation doesn't need to be its companion. We can choose to forgive our abusers while also disconnecting from them and the harm they continually cause.

Acceptance over Forgiveness

Rather than place so much emphasis on forgiveness, I think a better way toward healing involves acceptance—acceptance of our abusers' identity, what they have done to us, and their hardened hearts toward us. Whether or not we forgive them, we can accept them. Besides, forgiveness can actually be detrimental and foolish to offer. Consider:

- It is unwise to forgive a person who shows zero care or insight into the ways they hurt us and treat others.
- It is unwise to forgive a person who hurts us over and over again.
- It is even dangerous to forgive a person who shows no remorse for their actions, who can never admit wrong, and who would prefer to lose relationships than apologize and make things right.

Our toxic family members may give our grievances some lip service, but if they turn around and hurt us again, their words are hollow and void of integrity. The reality is, we do not have to forgive someone who repeatedly abuses and disrespects us, smears our character, and does all they can to damage other significant relationships in our life. Forgiveness under these conditions can only result in our own demise. We will be left with no self-respect, zero confidence, and an inability to count on ourselves to make good decisions.

Healing Moment

In place of forgiveness, what we can do to heal is accept our toxic family members for exactly who they are without expecting, wishing, or hoping for them to be different.

Forgiveness does not always equate to reconciliation. Sometimes forgiveness means we accept an abuser for their abusive nature, set ourselves free from them, and set them free to be the abusive people they are. There are times in life when the most important thing we can do is come to understand that, in some relationships, it's simply better to be free. This means we let go, we move on, and we never look back. This is what I mean by acceptance. It is the mindful way to heal from reprehensible acts. We don't have to forgive unacceptable acts upon us. Nor does that make us unhealthy or bad. I think it makes us smart and self-loving and acknowledges us as persons of intrinsic value.

Whether we choose to forgive or not, when wrongs have been done to us, to be healthy we have to accept that these horrible things were done. We have to accept that these hurtful things were immensely damaging to us and were perpetrated again and again regardless of how obvious our hurt was. We don't have to like what has happened to us, and we can wish that the hurts didn't happen, but we cannot change them or deny their reality.

When we come to accept our toxic family members for exactly who they are, we get into the reality of our situation and the anger, rage, and other emotions which come along with it. As we create the necessary space to feel our emotions, they slowly diminish. We start to accept our hurt and damaged feelings as a healthy and natural part of our recovery. We adapt to and assimilate the totality of what we endured under our toxic family members.

We suffer the most and build the "emotional prison" people speak of only when we resist accepting what has happened to us. We suffer because we want the reality of our toxic family members to be other than what it is. But with acceptance, we learn that no amount of avoidance, fighting, forgiveness, or denial can change our circumstances or the twisted people who created those circumstances.

Acceptance is what has brought me the peace I've needed to feel and the ability to rise above the small thinking of others when it comes to forgiveness. Acceptance brought me to a higher and healthier perspective. My toxic family members are who they are. I can accept knowing that I don't like them. When we can accept something, possibilities open up, as do healthier perceptions about what will be best for us going forward.

We all have a right to protect ourselves against the aggression of others, even when those who seek to harm us are family. Our toxic family members have persistently and ruthlessly harmed us in a host of ways. And no matter what we have done to seek to please them and honor them, they have chosen not to treat us in kind. And they have given us no genuine, trustworthy signs of ever treating us differently. Why, then, should we forgive them? They have given us no indication that they will act differently toward us, that they will finally stop hurting us and start loving us. And why should we keep putting ourselves in harm's way by trying to reconcile ourselves with them? They don't want reconciliation. That would require their recognition that they hurt us, that they need to treat us differently, and that they will, in fact, treat us as we should be treated—as valuable human persons worthy of love and care. They just want us around so they can keep hurting us, using us, manipulating us, damaging us … and all for their selfish ends. We may want peaceful coexistence with them, but they will have none of that. Two thousand years ago, the missionary and apostle Paul of Tarsus wrote, "If possible, so far as it depends on you, be at peace with all men."[48] Well, we have done all we can to be at peace with our toxic family members, and they only want ongoing conflict. So it's time for us to be done with them and stop the abuse, at least in our lives. This is the only way we will find peace.

Healing Moment

With acceptance, healing is about the victim. With forgiveness, healing is about the perpetrator.

The Joy and Pain of Life's Major Transitions

Recovery in life is always about being in transition. Transitions are the gray areas where we have to let go of the old and scramble to find and redefine what is new. It is during the grayness of our transitions that we experience the most pain and confusion. Here is where it is difficult to remain hopeful.

However, if we don't transition, we cannot change our lives for the better. Instead, we will run in place. Growing requires that we embrace the changes we've been forced to make to protect and save our life and liveliness. We need to be gentle with ourselves by taking whatever time we need to allow ourselves to adapt and adjust to all the changes along the way. This is no easy task.

When we start living our lives without the negative influence of our toxic family members, it can feel as if we no longer have roots. The family we grew up in was our sense of rootedness, at least in theory. It was the only sense of anchorage and settledness we had, even if it wasn't real.

In my own recovery, I have had to make my own roots. After a painful period of picking all the wrong romantic partners who only provided me with the familiar chaos of my family, I found myself single in my early forties. I took advantage of this transition and focused solely on creating a new and more stable life for myself. This involved purchasing my first house. This place was mine. I didn't get it through a divorce and did not have any financial assistance from my family. This home provided me with a protective sanctuary. I finally had something my toxic family members didn't have a hand in. Nothing about my home could be used against me for manipulation. I had landed in this place—my safe, cozy, loving environment that felt secure and pure. I finally had a place to call home. I had solid earth to step on that was void of landmines. I had a refuge where I could heal and nurture myself through this major transition of cutting ties with my toxic family members. In some ways, my home provides me with the emotional experience of being held, being safe, and being contained but not imprisoned. I never experienced any of this in my own family while growing up.

Our transitions are where we develop and create our new sense of self. We must consistently remind ourselves that we didn't separate from our toxic family members to hurt them. We did it to protect ourselves. As we recover, we find ways to repurpose our lives, to redefine our sense of value and personal significance by resetting our priorities. I believe what God wants for us is the individual freedom to express ourselves as fully and authentically in his world as we can.

After I cut ties with my mother, I got into therapy with a therapist who was well educated and knowledgeable on personality disorders. I went to her each week, and she helped to confirm my experience and all that I was learning through the reading I was doing. I am also an avid journal writer. Quite honestly, writing in my journal is probably what saved my life throughout my childhood and still saves me today. I have repeatedly written my way through terror to triumph. When I journal, I feel connected to the intimate conversation that is ongoing inside of me. My journal is the one place where I can be completely authentic. It heals me. My journal provides me with all of the conversations I have ever needed to have with the toxic people in my life who couldn't offer me a fair, equal, or loving relationship or conversation in return.

When we transition in our lives, the person we must find is who we are on the inside. And the love we must find is the love inside of ourselves. We have to examine the person in the mirror and the totality of the journey we have been through and come to feel love and pride in that beautiful person who is us.

Healing Moment

The most beautiful people we have known are those who have known defeat, suffering, struggle, and loss, and have found their way out of the depths. These persons have an understanding of life that fills them with compassion, gentleness, and a deep, loving concern.

—*Elisabeth Kübler-Ross*

Lyric Therapy

You can stand me up at the gates of hell
But I won't back down ...

No, I'll stand my ground
Won't be turned around
—"I Won't Back Down," by Tom Petty and the Heartbreakers[49]

13

Love Yourself and Change Your Life

The path to long-lasting healing requires love. And the work to define, know, and experience love starts with you.

If you want healthy love, you must be healthy first.

Loving yourself means getting to know who you are and never accepting treatment that is less than respectful toward you.

Healing Moment

Healing is the result of love. It is a function of love. Wherever there is love there is healing. And, wherever there is no love there is precious little—if any—healing. The psychology of evil must be a loving psychology. It must be brimful of the love of life. Every step of the way its methodology must be submitted not only to the love of truth but also to the love of life: of warmth and light and laughter, and spontaneity and joy and service and human caring.[50]

—Scott Peck

What Do You Know about Love?

When we've been raised in the fake-love environment where our family didn't fight for us or protect us but rather consistently and persistently fought against us for being who we are, love doesn't feel like love. We learn that love hurts. Likewise, children learn to respect themselves by how respectfully their parents treated them. If we weren't treated with respect, we didn't learn how to respect ourselves. It is this lack of respect for ourselves that has caused us to end up in all kinds of relationships with toxic people as adults. We unconsciously choose unhealthy connections of all kinds. The more we attract these dynamics, the more we believe there has to be something inherently wrong with us, so we keep repeating the pattern of trying to change ourselves to secure the love and acceptance of others.

We must come to understand and accept that love is a partnership that functions around the concepts of mutuality and reciprocity. The relationship is not swayed unfairly to meeting the needs of only one person. Love doesn't threaten or demand. Love is soft and easy. There is space given for each person's needs for their own individuality and independence. Love doesn't keep score. When we love and are loved in return, needs are forecasted and prepared for. Sacrificing for our partner is second nature. When love is authentic, the sacrifices we make for our partner don't create exhaustion or resentments because we are sacrificed for in like measure.

Healing Moment

 Love doesn't hurt people. Toxic people hurt people.

When we are with others who are not whole, we spend so much time trying to build them up that we sacrifice all that is healthy for us. This never works long-term. If we cannot be who we need to be in our relationships, we end up existing in an unfair and oppressive emotional prison. Relationships cannot sustain if they are only one-way. If we allow ourselves to stay in one-way relationships, we are contributing to our own demise. We must hold the mind-set that we deserve the best, that we deserve to feel good about who we are instead of constantly questioning if we're good enough. We must hold a caring concern for ourselves, not just for other people. We must care about ourselves to make ourselves our top priority. We do this by doing for ourselves all the things we so generously do for others. We deserve this.

When we love ourselves, all other healthy relationships sprout from there. Therefore, the most significant person to love in our lives must always be ourselves. It is too easy to lose track of loving ourselves when we're focused on loving the wrong people. We get pulled away from what we love, who we love, our careers, friendships … everything. It's a terrible way to live because we become disconnected from our own desires, trying to keep up with who we think these toxic people want us to be. We have to get back to ourselves, to our lives, to our authenticity. When we start loving ourselves, we take ourselves back from the people who have been hurtful to us.

Love should not be hurtful; it should be helpful. Love appreciates and acknowledges. Love doesn't hide, lie, or conceal. It is open and vulnerable. When love is present, there is a commitment to travel through the harder times of life with as much honesty, integrity, and teamwork as possible. If what we're living doesn't reflect this, then we must question if what we have is love. The key to understanding what we have is to look objectively at how we feel the majority of the time. If we are worn out and depleted, we simply deserve better. We are the only people who can get ourselves to an improved and fulfilling life, and that comes through making some difficult changes. We must see ourselves and our future as well worth those changes.

Healing Moment

 The main goal in loving ourselves must be geared toward moving on, not going back.

We must commit to taking steps forward. We must focus compassionately on ourselves, on rebuilding our own sense of value and worth, and kick out the feelings of loneliness and anxiety that we were conditioned to feel in these negative, manipulative, and imprisoning toxic family dynamics. Getting out of these dynamics is a courageous act of self-love.

I needed love after I cut ties so I hired my therapist and a business coach to help me. Between these two supports, I was able to get on my feet emotionally and create more opportunities for me and my business. I chose a female to be my therapist and a male to be my business coach. Because I lack connection with both a mother and a father, I chose these two people to be surrogates for me. They helped me stay gathered and to heal my pain. They also supported my need to believe in myself again. I have learned so much from both of them. I have learned how to be loved in the right way and how to slow my relationships down. As I've healed I have begun to see that there are other good people out there just like me. I have learned to allow myself to love and be loved again and in all the healthy ways I crave and deserve. With my supports in place, I attracted more and more amazing people and opportunities. I left the drama, the manipulative games, and my abusers behind. I have risen up and continue to move forward.

Healing Moment

 Leave toxic people where they belong—in your past.

You Don't Owe Anyone Anything

Sometimes it is hard for us to know how to meet our own needs coming from toxic family dynamics because the only needs we were ever meeting were those of our abusers. This is one of the reasons I commit to therapy. It is my responsibility to make sure that I am too full of life to be half-loved. I have to be the one person who can fill my life up in all the ways I want. I set goals for myself and put them up on a corkboard. I find my happiness through working hard, embracing my passions, and wisely choosing the company I keep. I have learned that not everyone deserves to be my friend, not everyone deserves to know my heart, and not everyone deserves to have a relationship with me. The better I treat myself, the healthier I am as a person, the more whole I feel, and the more I attract all these great qualities in others.

When I made the decision to fully commit to my happiness by establishing no contact with my toxic family members and the many other toxic people I had been hosting, I stopped allowing anyone to get in the way of my doing what I needed to do to be happy. I have learned that I have far more power inside of me than I had ever imagined. With my toxic family members in their proper place, my life isn't nearly as scary, painful, or confusing anymore. I have paid my dues far and above in those relationships. I owe them nothing. This is a beautiful feeling.

Get Your Dignity Back

We lose our worth and dignity when we continue to host our negative family members. They are not going to magically show up one day and be who we want them to be. Our mind-set needs to be focused solely on healing ourselves. Each day we wait for karma to catch up to our toxic family members is another day of our life we've wasted thinking about them. We can trust that their day will come, but we must not put our own lives on pause to sit and anxiously wait for it. That day is not under our control; it's under the control of the laws of cause and effect.

In the meantime, getting our dignity back starts by focusing on ourselves and all the choices we now have the freedom to make to heal our heart, our mind, and our spirit. As we rebuild our life, we will get to the place where the consequences of our abusers' actions finally do catch up to them. This will come to us as a sweet and unexpected surprise. It will serve to enhance our trust in God, in fate, in what is right and fair, and in our decision to cut ties with toxic people.

In her book *My Story*, Elizabeth Smart wrote about the horror she experienced when she was kidnapped and tortured. After she finally returned home, her mother gave her some wise advice regarding the people who harmed her: "You may never feel like justice has been served or that true restitution has been made. But don't you worry about that. At the end of the day, God is our ultimate judge. He will make up to you every pain and loss that you have suffered. And if it turns out that these wicked people are not punished here on earth, it doesn't matter. His punishments are just. You don't ever have to worry. You don't ever have to think about them again."[51] I cannot read these words without tearing up. I may not have been tortured as Elizabeth was, but she has something I do not and that is a family who loves her, supports her, and holds her up. And yet, I can still move forward knowing that justice is ultimately in God's hands; he will confront my toxic family in his time and in his way. In the meantime, I can move on.

Since I have chosen the path of silence with my toxic family members, I have witnessed my life blessed with incredible increase and favor that have extended far beyond my wildest dreams. I feel certain there is no God punishing me for my decision to love and protect myself. He has always wanted those things for me. Instead I realize more than ever that our toxic family members are no longer worthy of our time, energy, or focus because we are putting all of that into the healing of our wounds. The most important thing we can do to help us rebuild the love we have for ourselves is to educate ourselves on the patterns and ways of toxic people. I cannot tell you how many great books, many that I have referenced here, have helped to save my life, to heal my heart, and to get me pointed firmly in the right direction—away from my toxic family.

I protect my life fiercely because I've worked so hard to create my freedom. The research repeatedly shows our toxic family members will never change. So if change is to occur, it must be mine to achieve. *I have to change.*

You Do You

We do not owe anyone an explanation for why we will not tolerate the intolerable. We simply must not tolerate it anymore. We make our decision to cut ties, and we live it for the truth that it is. We cannot live a fulfilling life waiting on the approval of others. If we don't make the decisions we need to live happily, the life we want will never manifest. We are the ultimate decision-makers and owners of our lives, and we must let others know where they stop and where we start. The decisions we make must be in line with what we need to feel emotionally safe and happy.

Anyone who hovers over every aspect of our lives is not loving us; that person is seeking to control us. Control is not love, and it is not respect. And when such people call us unappreciative or disrespectful for taking the steps we need for our own recovery and healing, they are not standing on firm ground. We, however, are. We are standing on the solid rock of our personal rights and intrinsic value as human beings.

We must not look for toxic people to support us or have our backs. We do not need their permission to be who we need to be, who we desire to be, or who we deserve to be. Freedom is our own personal right, not something to be dictated by others. I have fully embraced that I have every right to make any decision I need to make to protect myself from intolerable treatment. Our toxic family members will tell us we're selfish anytime we take charge, but we do not need to put up with their bullish ways, criticisms, and other forms of manipulation.

Is it selfish to take care of myself? No!

Is it selfish to protect myself? No!

When someone has the full-blown agenda to beat me down, to find something, anything, that is wrong with me, and to tell me I am selfish when I finally blow up and set boundaries because I've reached my limit, the problem is not with me. Standing up for my rights against poor treatment isn't selfish—it is appropriate, healthy self-care. I have learned if I don't take care of myself, no one else will and no one else can. Self-care all starts with the person I see each day in the mirror. I need to come first. I need to nurture myself, care for myself, have passions, friends, eat healthy, and have people to love who love me in return. I am not a bad person. I now know I deserve to be loved, and I am finally attracted to loving people.

Take care of yourself. You do you. If you really learn to love yourself, you will gain the capacity to truly love others. Even Jesus said that one of the greatest commandments given in the Bible is to love your neighbor *as yourself.*[52] Neighbor-love is predicated on self-love.

Honor Yourself

One of the greatest things about life is we can start over as many times as we need to. We can make mistake after mistake and commit to learning from each one. Each mistake can give us a deeper wisdom to operate from when making future decisions.

Life is all about examining ourselves. This type of self-examination helps us maximize our strengths and develop new ones.

Moreover, it is up to us to know our value and refuse to accept treatment that ranks far below the value we hold for ourselves. We must discipline ourselves not to focus our efforts on wishing our toxic family members would change. We must put our efforts at healing toward loving ourselves, changing our patterns, and honoring who we are. That's power. If we're treated poorly, we are allowing it, and that is the pattern we have to fix. Is this hard? Yes, it is incredibly hard. But the bigger question is, Is it worth it? If we want to live a life we love, if we want to love and be loved, then the answer to this question is undoubtedly yes. The greatest gift we give ourselves is to live a life that feels like it truly is our choice. When we are caught in toxic relationships, it feels as if we lost personal ownership of our life and handed it over to someone else. When a toxic relationship is running our life, we cannot recover. We live in a state of helplessness and question if we can or will ever get our control back—not control over the other people but taking away *their* control over our life. The only life we can control or even should is our own. Healing involves recognizing this truth and moving forward with it firmly embedded in our psyche and will.

Healing means taking responsibility for our life. It means removing shame and fear for doing what we know is in our best interest. For me it meant looking out for myself at the great risk of others not liking or accepting me for who I am. I've learned to say "So what!" to my naysayers because they've not walked a mile in my shoes. I have the courage and patience to let people show me who they really are. Holding this type of patience and objectivity allows me to move on in my life and to replace the negative, judgmental, disingenuous people with positive, genuine people. I remove the gossips from my life. I get rid of the people who thrive on whatever drama is going on that is somehow connected to me. Likewise, I encourage you to get them out of your life as well. They serve you nothing. They contribute nothing of value. Gossips are not in our life to love us but to look in on us and report back to our toxic family members. They share what we're doing and interpret what they see with their own twist of drama on it. If we host these types of two-faced people, we invite a miserable life. Instead we must free ourselves, love ourselves, and choose to live peacefully ever after at least as much as it depends on us.

Healing Moment

 Self-love is setting boundaries.

The Gift of Walking Away

When we remove toxic people from our lives, our lives transform.

At first, walking away feels miserable, as if we're going cold turkey from an addiction. The good news is that time heals. After letting go, we will see with each passing day that we experience more and more unexpected blessings. We begin to develop our self-respect as we hold our boundaries. We regain our ability to think rationally and to feel joy again. Instead of running frantically around trying to avoid conflict and feeling full of anxiety, we start spending time with people who do not treat us in ways that require us to constantly explain ourselves. This type of self-created freedom allows our spirit to thrive.

As we continue to heal, we will look back one day with complete bewilderment as to how we even tolerated interacting with such manipulative people in the first place. Our new self grows to feel protective of our old self, and this, my friends, is an immensely beautiful place to be.

So my counsel to you is …

- Be good to yourself.
- Be proud of yourself.
- Remind yourself of how far you've come and all that you have come through.
- Remind yourself of all the times you've pushed through even when you had every doubt in the world that you would not make it.
- Remind yourself of all the mornings that it felt too hard to get out of bed, to get through another day, but you did it anyway.

- Remind yourself that you're a warrior, that you have worth, and that you will doggedly refuse to let anyone take you for granted.
- Remind yourself of all the wisdom you've developed through your trials that now serve as weapons and strategies to keep you safe, happy, and healthy.
- Remind yourself that you're a work in progress.
- Remind yourself that all of this is a beautiful thing.

You CAN

You *can*.

You can be whoever you want, do what you want, live your dream, find ways to solve your problems, and find love and peace within yourself and in your relationships.

You can breathe and live without your toxic family members. This can seem incredibly hard, but this is because we get stuck in toxic situations and relationships and become blinded to our freedom, to how strong we are, and most importantly, we lose our sense of worth. We ultimately start to believe life is not under our direction but under that of another. When we start putting consistent effort into ourselves, we will overcome this lie and we will heal.

Feelings of being stuck are real feelings, but they are just feelings. They are not reality! In reality we are never stuck. There is no entrance into our healing as long as we do not have control over our own life decisions. Self-love is crucial for a happy life because there is often no one else who will be there for us exactly when we need them. But *you* will always be there. And yet, we spend so much time craving other people. Other people are certainly necessary, and most will be there whenever they can, but at the end of the day, we still have to travel our pain alone. We must come to learn the difference between being by ourselves and being with ourselves. Every time we hurt and every time we succeed, we have the opportunity to nurture ourselves and to celebrate ourselves in the ways others have failed to do.

When we learn to re-parent or re-love ourselves in the ways we've always deserved, we develop a resilience within that will change our life. We become a better lover of others. We also become easier to love because we aren't constantly needing from other people or living in total fear of them. When we can self-sustain, we can be just as happy in our own solitude as we are when connecting with other people. It's so important to learn to fill our own cup. When we fill our own cup, we never run out of the time, love, and attention we crave because we know how to give it to ourselves. This makes loving us so much more enjoyable for others, and it makes our experience of loving others more satisfying for us. When we're full from within, we're not constantly focused on what others are failing to do for us to be happy. We've got the happiness thing down without them. We can find whatever is missing from within ourselves. We also have more courage to tell others what we need, so they are better directed and equipped to love us in the ways we desire to be loved. The irony is this: The less we need from others, the more others feel compelled to give to us.

There are so many amazing, wonderful, loving, honest, kind, and healthy people in this world. The longer we host our toxic family members, the more we are blocked from anything new or better entering into our lives. I am blessed to have the most loving and incredible chosen family. I am happy to say that my chosen family has greatly expanded since I established no contact with the negative people in my life. I have my beautiful daughter, my best girlfriends, all of my patients, a huge Facebook following, my own therapist, my business coach, my acquisitions editor, my editor, my incredible boyfriend and his family, and my sweet pets. I couldn't be more blessed than I am right now.

I know God has seen my pain, has known my suffering, and has sent many angels my way to help me jump off the cliff into establishing no contact. I wear Saint Michael around my neck as a protector against evil, and I got a tattoo of a butterfly on my wrist (my lifeline) with the letters BTBF above it. It stands for Better To Be Free. I can say without any doubt that all I have lost has been replaced by the extraordinary. I am surrounded by people who love me, care about me, and support me. Not everyone in my chosen family knows my story. They are respectful of my privacy, which is new for me. It feels good to have my privacy respected. I feel safe. I feel loved. And most importantly, I feel deeply happy.

You can have all of this too. But it won't happen for you until you choose it. You must choose freedom over slavery.

You must choose to value yourself over your abusers.

You must choose health over harm.

You must choose a life of healing over hurting.

You must change.

The good news is that you can do all of these things. The world of manipulation, deceit, lies, degradation, and all the other destructive weapons your toxic family members have used against you can be left behind. You can remove them from your life. I have done this. And many others have done this too. What we have done, you can too.

Lyric Therapy

Leaving behind nights of terror and fear

I rise

Into a daybreak that's wondrously clear

I rise

—"Still I Rise," by Maya Angelou[53]

Acknowledgments

I would like to extend my gratitude to the Morgan James family for giving me a shot at my publishing dreams.

I want to thank Terry Whalin for following me on Twitter and for being open to hearing about me and my writing. I felt something so special in you, and I knew that your interests in me were genuine. From the second we talked, I knew you were on my team. I will never forget getting your call telling me that Morgan James Publishing was offering me a contract.

I want to thank Bill Watkins, my incredible editor. It's a truly magical experience to have an editor who gets who you are psychologically and who supports you through such an emotional and vulnerable process. There were times writing this book that my emotions were so intense that I had a hard time getting them out on paper. Bill stayed patient and compassionate toward me and knew exactly what I was trying to say. I thank you, Bill, for being on my team and for touching my heart and allowing it to be open.

I want to thank my beautiful daughter, London. London, you are my angel and my Why in life. You are my greatest and deepest blessing.

I want to thank Scott Holmes for your unfaltering love and support.

I want to thank all of my friends and my chosen family for loving me and inspiring me every day to be the best version of myself that I can be.

I want to thank all of the people who have hurt me. The hurt you have inflicted into my life forced me to deeply find, know, accept, and love myself. I have risen and will continue to rise inspired by you. Because of the barriers you placed in my way, I have come to trust the depth of my spirit and the beautiful resilience I have within me to overcome.

About the Author

Dr. Sherrie Campbell is a nationally recognized expert in clinical psychology, an inspirational speaker, former radio host of the *Dr. Sherrie Show* for the BBM Global Network and TuneIn Radio, an active writer for *Huffington Post* and Entrepreneur.com, and the author of *Success Equations: A Path to Living an Emotionally Wealthy Life*. Her blogs appear in nearly all sections of the *Huffington Post*, and she's one of the top read contributors for Entrepreneur.com. Dr. Sherrie is also a regularly featured expert on radio and television.

Dr. Sherrie was selected by the Beauty In Beauty Out Tour 2015 and received a Reflection Award in Los Angeles for being a Real Superwoman in her community. She received this award in acknowledgment for her dedication to freely providing love, support, advice, and motivation on her professional Facebook page (www.facebook.com/sherriecampbellphd). Fifteen elite women in the state of California were chosen for this acknowledgment. She is now a current board member for the Beauty In Beauty Out Foundation.

Dr. Sherrie earned her PhD in 2003 and is a licensed psychologist with over two decades of clinical training experience providing counseling and psychotherapy services to residents of Orange County in California. She not only works with patients in her private practice but also mentors and shares her expertise with others throughout the United States and worldwide, providing sessions via phone call or Facetime. In her private practice, she specializes in psychotherapy with adults and teenagers, including providing marriage and family therapy and counseling for grief, childhood trauma, sexual issues, personality disorders, illness, and more. Dr. Sherrie has helped individuals manage their highest highs and survive their lowest lows—from winning the lottery to the death of a child. Her interactive sessions are as unique and impactful as is her first book, *Loving Yourself: The Mastery of Being Your Own Person.*

She is the mother of a daughter who inspires her every move in life. Dr. Sherrie is also an avid athlete, and she loves her alone time to read and write in her journal.

Also by Dr. Sherrie Campbell

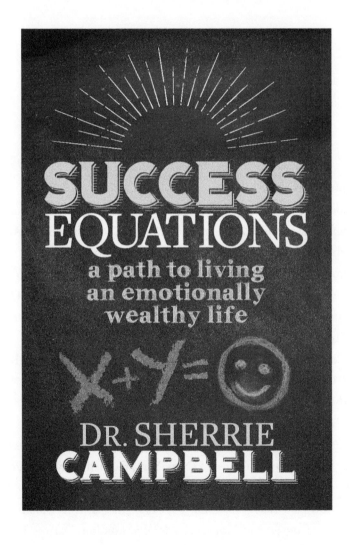

Endnotes

1 @allthings_possible.

2 Shahida Arabi, *Becoming the Narcissist's Nightmare: How to Devalue and Discard the Narcissist While Supplying Yourself* (New York: SCW Archer Publishing, 2016), n.p.

3 Shannon Thomas, *Healing from Hidden Abuse: A Journey through the Stages of Recovery from Psychological Abuse* (Mast Publishing House, 2016), n.p.

4 M. Scott Peck, *People of the Lie: The Hope for Healing Human Evil* (New York: Touchstone, 1983), 43–44.

5 Katy Perry, vocalist, "By The Grace of God," by Greg Wells and Katy Perry, *Prism*, Capitol Records, 2013.

6 This thought was inspired by the writings of Shannon Thomas.

7 Peck, *People of the Lie*, 60.

8 Virginia Satir, as quoted in Peter L. Rudnytsky, *Reading Psychoanalysis: Freud, Rank, Ferenczi, Groddeck* (New York: Cornell University Press, 2002), 44.

9 Danu Morrigan, *You're Not Crazy—It's Your Mother: Understanding and Healing for Daughters of Narcissistic Mothers* (London: Darton, Longman and Todd Ltd., 2012), 50.

10 Lindsay C. Gibson, *Adult Children of Emotionally Immature Parents: How to Heal from Distant, Rejecting, or Self-Involved Parents* (Oakland: New Harbinger Publications, 2015), 9.

11 Sia, vocalist, "Alive," by Adele, Tobias Jesso Jr., and Sia, *This Is Acting*, Universal Music Publishing and EMI Music Publishing, 2015.

12 Brenda Hunter, *The Power of Mother Love: Strengthening the Bond between You and Your Child* (Colorado Springs: Waterbrook Press, 1997), n.p.

13 Cindi Lopez, "Narcissistic Mothers," PsychCentral, March 15, 2017, https://psychcentral.com/lib/narcissistic-mothers.

14 Eminem, vocalist, "Cleaning Out My Closet," by Jeff Bass and Eminem, *The Eminem Show*, Ensign Music Corp. (BMI)/Eight Mile Style (BMI), 2002.

15 See thenarcissisticlife.com.

16 NF, vocalist, "Let You Down," by Tommee Profitt and NF, *Perception*, Caroline Records, NF Real Music LLC, and Capitol Records, 2017.

17 Kesha, vocalist, "Praying," by Andrew Joslyn, Ben Abraham, Ryan Lewis, and Kesha, *Rainbow*, Kemosabe Records, 2017.

18 Carolyn Steber, "7 Signs You Have a Toxic Sibling," *Bustle*, January 27, 2016, https://www.bustle.com/articles/138082-7-signs-you-have-a-toxic-sibling.

19 Elton John, vocalist, "I'm Still Standing," by Bernie Taupin, *Too Low for Zero*, Geffen Records and The Rocket Record Co., 1983.

20 Tom Petty, vocalist, "Wildflowers," by Tom Petty, *Wildflowers*, Warner Brothers, 1994.

21 Morrigan, *You're Not Crazy—It's Your Mother*, n.p.

22 Marwa Eltagouri, "A 30-Year-Old Demanded Notice for Eviction from His Parents' House," *The Washington Post*, May 22, 2018, https://www.washingtonpost.com/news/post-nation/wp/2018/05/22/a-30-year-old-demanded-six-month-notice-for-eviction-from-his-parents-house-a-judge-called-that-outrageous/?noredirect=on&utm_term=.5f563528a607.

23 Dua Lipa, vocalist, "IDGAF," by Whiskey Waters, Larzz Principator, Skyler Stonestreet, MNEK, and Dua Lipa, *Dua Lipa*, TaP Music Publishing Ltd. et al, 2017.

24 Adele, vocalist, "Turning Tables," by Ryan Tedder and Adele, *21*, Columbia Records and XL Recordings, 2011.

25 Proverbs 17:13.

26 Sister Renee Pittelli, *The Christian's Guide to No Contact: How to End Your Relationships with Narcissistic, Psychopathic, and Abusive Family and Friends, and Still Be a Good Christian* (CreateSpace Independent Publishing Platform, 2017), 8.

27 Ibid., 43.

28 In support, see Joseph's story in Genesis 37–50; see also Psalm 40:1–5, 11–15; James 5:10–11.

29 In the Old Testament, for example, God tells the Hebrews to purge the Promised Land of its evil inhabitants as they prepare to live there (Deuteronomy 6:10–19; 7:1–11). And Proverbs urges its readers to avoid the way of the wicked (Proverbs 4:14–19). In the New Testament, examples include Jesus driving out by force the money-changers in the Temple area (John 2:13–16), and the apostle Paul telling the Christians in Corinth to distance themselves from the immoral people in their midst (1 Corinthians 5:11) and to excommunicate a man engaged in incest (vv. 1–7).

30 Bruno Mars, vocalist, "Treasure," by The Smeezingtons, Bruno Mars, and Phredley Brown, *Unorthodox Jukebox*, Atlantic Records, 2012.

31 See the book of Job, for example. What evil took from him God eventually restored and even doubled (Job 1–2; 42:10–17). The book of Ruth also tells the story of how two widows receive restoration and added blessing in unexpected ways.

32 For example, see the story about Pharaoh and the Exodus, especially how this ruler hardened his heart no matter what happened to him or his people (Exodus 5–14). See also Psalm 37:12–15, 35–38; Proverbs 4:14–19; 6:12–15; 17:11; 21:7, 10.

33 Ephesians 4:32; Colossians 3:13.

34 See Ezekiel 33:10–19; Isaiah 55:6–7; Acts 3:19.

35 See Jeremiah 6:16–21; 22:3–5; Luke 13:3, 5. For more, go to Sister Renee Pittelli's website, www.Luke13:3Ministries.com.

36 See 1 Kings 8:33–40, 46–50; Acts 8:14–24; 1 John 1:5–10.

37 See, for instance, Psalm 7:12–16; Jeremiah 5–6; 8:1–17; Ezekiel 14:1–8; Revelation 2:19–23.

38 See Ezekiel 18:20–32; Luke 3:7–14; Acts 26:20; Revelation 2:2–5.

39 Matthew 18:23–34, NASB.

40 Matthew 5:44.

41 John 2:23–24.

42 Thomas, *Healing from Hidden Abuse*, 37.

43 Blue Foundation, "Eyes on Fire," *Life of a Ghost*, EMI and Astralwerks, 2007.

44 Gibson, *Adult Children of Emotionally Immature Parents*, 11.

45 R. P. L. Bowlby et al, *The Making and Breaking of Affectional Bonds* (New York: Routledge, 1979, 2005).

46 Demi Lovato, vocalist, "Warrior," by FRND, Lindy Robbins, Demi Lovato, and Emanuel Kiriakou, *Demi*, Hollywood Records, 2013.

47 Romans 10:8–10.

48 Romans 12:18, NASB.

49 Tom Petty and the Heartbreakers, "I Won't Back Down," by Jeff Lynne and Tom Petty, *Full Moon Fever*, Geffen Records and MCA Records, 1989.

50 Peck, *People of the Lie*, 44.

51 Elisabeth Smart with Chris Stewart, *My Story* (New York: St. Martin's Press, 2013), n.p.

52 Matthew 22:39.

53 Maya Angelou, "Still I Rise," in Maya Angelou, *And Still I Rise: A Book of Poems* (New York: Random House, 1978), https://www.poetryfoundation.org/poems/46446/still-i-rise.

Printed in the USA
CPSIA information can be obtained
at www.ICGtesting.com
JSHW021507220424
61657JS00004B/29